Gold & Silver
Is Honest Money

Top 21 Most Asked Questions
about Gold and Silver

Answered in 30 Minutes

DAMION S. LUPO

If you're interested in precious metal investing, this book is literally a gold mine! Damion gives you the dos and don'ts of investing in precious metals and a clear understanding why now is the time to invest in gold and silver. He removes the veil that the banking system and government have covered our eyes with so that we can understand and capitalize on the true meaning of wealth. If you want to protect your wealth from inflation or build your wealth through gold and silver, this book is a MUST READ.

—Peter Scott IV
Author & Speaker – the Fearless Academy

I have known and worked with Damion for over 10 years. He does what he says he will do, and what he does from an education and service perspective is of tremendous value to investors in the gold and silver markets.

—Keith J. Cunningham Author
Speaker, Educator, DecaMillionaire

Gold & Silver is Honest Money is a crash course in the fundamentals of investing in gold and silver. Never before have we come across such a wealth of knowledge presented in a clear and concise reference piece. Damion Lupo is disseminating information that we have yet to see in print anywhere else. We had to learn these lessons the hard way. Now, if it only came with a time machine so that we could go back and do it the right way the first time.

—K. Robinson and B. Robinson
Entrepreneurs

Gold & Silver is Honest Money

Inquiries should be addressed to:
Opul Enterprises Ltd.
PO Box 1930
Sedona, AZ 86339

www.MyGoldAdvisor.com

First Edition
First Printing October 12, 2012
Second Printing October 6, 2013

Edited by: Rick Lewis
Cover design by: Cornelia Murariu
Layout design by: Jake Muelle

ISBN   978-0-9764754-2-2   print
ISBN   978-0-9764754-3-9   electronic

1. Precious Metals 2. Retirement Accounts 3. Investments

Sections: BUSINESS / PERSONAL FINANCE / INVESTING

- Author's Note -

This book is designed to provide general information pertaining to the subjects discussed including, gold, silver and retirement accounts. Laws and general practices vary from state to state and change constantly.

Different, specific advice for those situations should be obtained by the reader's own advisors pertaining to the reader's situation.

The author has taken reasonable precautions in preparing this book and believes the facts are accurate as of the date it was written. Many of the thoughts, ideas and opinions are subjective and relevant to the current environment. They could change based any number of evolving environments, laws and geo political shifts. Neither the author nor publisher assume any responsibility for any errors or omissions. The author and publisher specifically disclaim any liability resulting from the use or application of the information contained in this book, and the information is not intended to serve as legal advice related to individual situations.

The author highly recommends you consult with your advisors, including your attorney and accountant about any plans you may have or are considering and that you get their professional opinion and advice before taking any action.

This book is dedicated to the two people who inspired my quest for knowledge in precious metals that ultimately became this book.

Marc Watts & Kirk Robinson

You two are an inspiration and a big reason the truth in this book now shines on the world. Thank you for your honesty, your guidance and your friendship these years and for pushing me to always find more ways to serve.

To my clients and friends. May you find safety in real things and trust in the people you share your life with.

Table of Contents

PART II: WHY NOW?

PART IV: TOP 7 SCAMS

- Introduction -

If gold and silver are so awesome, why don't Suze, Dave and my financial advisor recommend them?

The most common question I've received over the last couple years is from friends and clients who ask me why they should own gold and silver, since their financial adviser hasn't recommended it and sometimes has even recommended against it. They listen to Suze and Dave on the radio pushing mutual funds as the best path toward being "diversified" and urging them to have six months of reserves in cash. Rarely, if ever, do these celebrity financial experts encourage their listeners to purchase precious metals, and they've certainly been known to discourage it.

What they're really asking is, "Why would the mainstream financial industry, including my own advisor, push me away from gold and silver?"

The first thing to understand is mutual fund companies, Wall Street, and the banking industry pay to advertise in print magazines like *Money*, *Kiplinger's*, etc., and they also support many of the expert radio personalities through advertising. Advertising dollars are vital to their income and continued success. Long story short: These folks aren't going to bite the hand that feeds them.

The financial advisors you meet in your daily life are generally well intentioned, but they're focused on convincing you that the financial world is far too complex for the average person like you. Financial decisions, they say, should be left to the experts.

To be fair, they are often experts in what they know. But on average they only know the financial tools and strategies that require a financial advisor to manage them for you. Many will only use their tool bucket of products they're selling and will rarely suggest you take your money and invest it somewhere else. How could they stay in business if they recommended you take your money away from them and invest in something outside of their management? That would be biting their own hand. They must sell something to make a living.

In most cases, a financial industry expert advisor has a limited selection of products to solve their clients' problems. The products they have are all paper products (mutual funds, annuities, insurance, stocks, etc.) created by Wall Street and requiring all sorts of fees and commissions. Many of those products are great...for the brokers and the financial firms.

In the late 1990s, I owned an insurance and financial services firm in Gilbert, Arizona. As a financial advisor, I saw firsthand how the system worked and who profited from it. My parent company pushed us to sell as much life insurance as possible and as many annuities as possible. They did this because these products were highly profitable. When I really dug in and studied the mechanics of the products we had to sell, I realized the greatest value in them was the profits to the company and commissions earned by the advisor. In many cases the products were not in the client's best interest but many advisors, agents and brokers are only allowed to offer a limited selection of products, sort of keeping their hands tied.

I was one of those advisors, limited to a list of products and not allowed to offer outside options like gold and silver. In frustration for the limited scope of what I could do to protect my clients I resigned within a couple years.

Other than the rare exception, most financial advisors are narrowly focused on their limited offerings and will discourage their clients from looking at anything else. After all, outside investments aren't going to earn the advisor any fees and commissions.

A great way to find the truth when someone recommends one thing or discourages another is to ask where the money's flowing—in other words, what's in it for the advisor—if you do X or Y? If you buy physical gold and silver, the typical financial advisor will not make a dime and loses any control over that part of your investment portfolio. Naturally, they're not going to recommend this course of action.

It's entirely up to you to become educated about your finances and protect yourself. Relying on limited scope financial advisors or radio celebrities is a surefire way to keep your wealth locked up in a dangerously unstable Wall Street system and risk going broke.

Study, learn, and realize no one will ever care about your money more than you do.

PART I

Why Gold & Silver?

-1-

Why do I need gold and silver? What's better, silver or gold? Do silver and gold serve the same purpose or are they different?

QUICK:

You need gold and silver to protect your wealth. Why? Because it's real money. In fact, it's the only real money—today, just as it has been for 5,000 years.

Right now, you're being exposed to the manipulation and games that the bankers and traders play with your money on Wall Street. This exposure is setting you up to get hammered when the bubble in equities and bonds inevitably bursts.

Gold is being rapidly accumulated by central banks all over the world because they've lost faith in currency. Since 2009, Russia has bought a total of 500 tons of gold while China has bought thousands of tons. And it's not just America's economic and military rivals who no longer trust the U.S. dollar, either. In 2012, Switzerland's central bank quietly increased its gold holdings by nearly 25%.

They simply don't trust the U.S. dollar, and they know how valuable gold is as a store of wealth. The banks of the world know how to keep their money. You don't want to bet against them!

Silver, on the other hand, is becoming more and more rare every day as the stock of it is being consumed faster than it's being mined. Some experts predict we'll run out of silver in the next 10 years because of its expanding usages in high-tech manufacturing. Silver is truly a miracle metal and is used in everything from solar panels to cell phones, as well as a host of medical devices because of its antibacterial properties.

Surprisingly, silver is scarcer than gold. Silver reserves are estimated to be approximately 500 million ounces available above ground compared to around 2 billion ounces of gold. This alone makes silver something of an anomaly considering that gold is valued at 50 times the price of silver as in 2017.

DIRTY DETAILS:

GOLD: Gold is held by central banks all over the planet because of its nature as true money and because it has historically been used to back currency. There's wisdom in following the giant elephant as it stomps a path through the grass. The elephant here is the central banks, and they're stomping away—collecting, buying and storing gold at unprecedented levels.

The central banks of India, China, Russia and many other countries are accumulating millions of ounces of gold every month, which also means millions and millions of ounces are being pulled out of the market and placed in central banks for them to use it as a reserve, a hedge. Why? These countries don't trust the U.S. dollar anymore. They don't trust its value because the Federal Reserve is creating trillions of dollars out of thin air and diluting the value of dollars already in existence. Therefore, we're constantly seeing the things we buy cost more money. Those things aren't changing. It's the volume of dollars in the world economy that's changing.

A simple way of looking at it is to imagine if the entire economy consisted of $100 in circulation as the entire consumer population and 5 apples as all the products available in the market. If that's the case, then the 5 apples are going to cost $20 each. Now imagine the magic central bank creates another $100 out of thin air so the total currency climbs to $200, but we still have only 5 apples. Those apples are suddenly going to cost $40 each.

This is what's happening right now with the currency and why everything around us seems to be getting more expensive. The reason gold and silver keep going up is because the quantity of U.S. dollars in print is exploding and will continue to do so as central banks attempt to continue to stimulate the economy. Gold and silver are the ultimate hedge against print currency. The reason they're becoming so popular is because the other options that used to look safe—like stocks, bonds and treasuries—no longer make sense. Even cash used to make sense, but none of these are safe any longer because they're either in an inflated bubble or they're being destroyed by inflation as is the case with treasuries and cash.

I've been saying since 2012 when the first version of this book was published that in the next few years we'd see either the Chinese or Russian governments announce some type of gold standard. That's exactly what has happened in 2017. China is setting up a partially gold back Yuan to trade oil with. This is an attempt to undercut the United States' lock on all oil traded throughout the globe.

The U.S. government will not go back to a gold standard because this would hand cuff Congressional spending. If the dollar is in any way backed or tied to gold, Congress is limited to spending based on the gold reserves. The politicians would be constrained, unable to deficit spend on entitlement programs and endless wars through fiat currency printing.

The hundreds of trillions of dollars in entitlements already owed by the U.S. Government virtually prohibit it from going back on a gold standard without reneging on its promise to pay for things like Medicare, Medicaid and Social Security—not to mention the trillions of dollars in government pensions that millions of people are relying on.

One of the leading first-world governments is almost certain to return to some kind of gold standard, and the rest of the nations are going to have to follow suit. Why? Because their currency will be highly devalued if it's backed by nothing while a neighboring country's currency is backed by something real.

This will put massive pressure on the United States to reverse course with its spending and consider a partial gold backing even though the backing would put limitations on the ability of Congress to deficit spend as much as it wanted.

A partial gold backing would be something akin to saying that for every $4,000 in currency, we'll hold one tenth of an ounce of gold rather than the half ounce of gold required for 100% backing (based on the 2017 value for gold).

Regardless of which country acts first or how the U.S. chooses to react, the value of gold and silver will explode overnight when this event happens. **The only way to take advantage of this coming change is to be proactive and accumulate as much gold and silver as you can NOW**.

The U.S. dollar has been the world's reserve currency for nearly a century, but that monopoly is going to change. Gold, on the other hand, is respected everywhere on the planet. Those who own the gold will make the rules and will have the ability to maintain and expand their wealth. Those who don't own the gold will be at the mercy of those who do.

Gold is highly mobile. Small amounts representing vast wealth can be moved around easily. A million dollars' worth of gold is only about the size of two tissue boxes.

SILVER: Silver is the "sleeper," unnoticed and forgotten by most investors. In my mind, it's the big opportunity. Silver has been money even longer and more often than gold. Plus, silver is used in manufacturing everything from cell phones and solar panels to medical devices (because of its antibacterial properties). It's even used in a line of clothing at Lululemon!

Silver is used and then thrown away… At least right now it is. That's the primary difference between silver and gold. Eighty-five percent of all the gold that has ever been pulled out of the ground is still available in the form of jewelry, coins and bars. Gold gets recycled and effectively stays in circulation while the silver tied up in manufactured goods regularly ends up in the trash heap.

The fact is, we're using, consuming and throwing away more silver every year than we're pulling out of the ground. We're eating up our reserves of silver. The same is not true with gold.

Because of this, silver is highly undervalued and stands ready to explode in value over the next few years. I also believe this change will create massive volatility in silver prices over the next three to seven years.

I suspect gold will rise well past $10,000 an ounce by 2025. At the same time, silver is likely to rise and exceed $100 per ounce— more likely reaching $400 or $500 per ounce. These values are what I consider to be the most likely rational values. The actual price could end up much higher if metals go into a super bubble. The current levels for gold and silver are nowhere near a bubble yet.

This isn't some economic doomsday scenario; it's a natural change that's easy to see coming. Basic economics tells you exactly what's going to happen. Currency gets printed faster and faster—dollars, euros, yen, etc.—but the amount of gold and silver on the planet stays exactly the same. The more currency in print, the more currency it takes to exchange for gold and silver.

The uncertainty and global chaos will continue driving people towards the stability and certainty of gold and silver. If you think war will end and global peace will descend on the world soon, gold probably wouldn't make a ton of sense for you. But if you believe what we're seeing in the global economy today is likely to continue, gold and silver are likely to be a smart hedge for you.

SILVER VS. GOLD

SILVER: There is less investment grade silver available for investors than there is gold.

In 2017, there is only enough investment grade silver available for each person on earth to have one tenth of an ounce.

Silver is in everything; it's a miracle metal.

In addition to being money, Silver is the most electrically conductive, thermally conductive, and reflective metal on the planet.

GOLD: It's the only money that's never failed! In the 5,000-year history of people using gold as money, gold has maintained its value and purchasing power. Every currency eventually fails (see currency vs. money in Chapter 4).

Gold is completely private and portable.

In times of economic uncertainty and crisis, it's the safest store of wealth.

In 2017, there is only enough investment grade gold available for every person to have one third of an ounce.

Over and over throughout history, gold has been revalued to account for all the excess currency in circulation. If that were to happen today, the value of gold would be between $8,000 and $25,000 an ounce.

-2-

Why should I buy gold and silver? Is the price going up or down?

QUICK:

The U.S. government is spending and printing more money, and banks around the world are buying gold— which is increasing demand. As demand goes up, so does value. As the value of currency (especially the U.S. dollar) decreases, the best way to preserve your purchasing power is with gold.

DIRTY DETAILS:

Everybody should be buying gold and silver right now. The reason I say this is because they are the only investments that makes any sense given the current environment of money printing. The follow-up question is whether I think the price of gold and silver is going up or down.

Typically, we buy an investment if we think it's going to rise in value or produce some type of cash flow. Gold and silver don't produce cash flow so the only question is: will their price go up or down?

The price of these metals is directly impacted by the actions of two groups: Congress and the Federal Reserve. The price of gold and silver will likely move higher if Congress continues massive deficit spending and the Federal Reserve continues to print money through its stimulus programs.

Right now, Congress is spending money like it's going out of style, and the Federal Reserve is printing money through multi-trillion-dollar stimulus programs. The price of gold and silver is a direct reflection of how much currency is being printed and how much money the federal government is spending. Thus, the question of what gold and silver are going to do over the next few years is simple to answer.

If Congress balanced the federal budget and the Federal Reserve stopped printing, monetizing debt and/or doing the funky chicken dance with the people's money, I'd have a very different perspective than my highly positive outlook on gold and silver. Frankly, my perspective would probably be neutral at best on gold and silver, but so long as Congress keeps spending and the Federal Reserve keeps printing, we're going to keep seeing upward pressure on pricing.

As we saw in the $40 apple example above, if more currency keeps being printed, commodities will increase in direct proportion to the amount of currency available to buy that commodity. They're a direct reflection of the value of the currency.

It comes down to simple supply and demand. Central banks like the Federal Reserve, European Central Bank and the Japanese central bank are all accumulating gold. The reason is because they don't trust other assets, including the U.S. dollar and other currencies. Since there's a lot of buying going on, there is also a lot of pressure on the market to adjust the price of gold upwards.

When there is more competition for the same item, prices rise. And if the price goes down, it's because there's less demand. Right now, there is more and more demand. Even the Chinese government is encouraging its citizens to buy gold and silver and hold it themselves. There's a whole lot of Chinese people listening to their government. If you have one billion people thinking about buying a little bit of gold and a little bit of silver, that creates a lot of demand. Even if only a fraction of the population can buy a minimal amount per person, that is still millions of ounces. So, overall, I think in the next few years we will see a massive movement up in the price of gold.

If the value or perceived value of gold holds steady while the value of the dollar goes down, the price of gold relative to the dollar will rise. It's a function of the currency. It's because gold and silver really are gold and silver, while the dollar (or euro or yen) are just paper.

For example, if one dollar is worth three eggs today, the same dollar will eventually buy a single egg as more currency is printed, the result of stimulus programs and fiat currency. The egg hasn't changed. It's still an egg. But the paper currency has less purchasing power—66% less.

Likewise, gold and silver don't change, regardless of how many dollars get printed. What's happening is that the dollar is decreasing in value. Those dollars are being printed out of thin air, just as they have been since the U.S. abandoned the gold standard.

Since 2008 alone, the Federal Reserve has printed several trillion dollars out of thin air. The Federal Reserve prints this currency to try to stimulate the economy. In fairness, this sometimes works... at least for a little while.

Stimulating the economy by printing cash is kind of like stimulating the brain by taking heroine. Sure, the user feels great, getting high for a brief period. The problem is that unless the user keeps pumping more heroine into his system, he crashes and goes into withdrawal. Then again, if he keeps pumping heroine into his system, eventually the body shuts down completely, that isn't a solution. The Fed can't keep pumping cash into the system indefinitely like heroine, eventually the overdose of cash will shut down the system entirely. When the stimulus stops, the economic withdrawal will be a massive recession and deep deflationary depression.

If the stimulus continues indefinitely, eventually the user will overdose and die, which is what the Federal Reserve is in effect doing to the dollar, printing so much of it that the death of the dollar is imminent if the printing continues.

This market crash is inevitable. The Federal Reserve has simply supplied too much heroine in the form of cheap money with artificially low interest rates. The crash is going to create a lot of chaos, but ultimately, gold and silver will benefit from the crash, because they are real money.

For thousands of years these metals have been the asset that people used to protect themselves from chaos and governmental currency manipulation. They've been the most stable investment for people to rely on historically and will be again during this coming shakeout.

-3-

Why are gold and silver inherently valuable? What makes gold better money than dollars and other currency?

QUICK:

G old and silver have the five keys of money and serve the three functions of money (see Chapter 4). Dollar bills, on the other hand, are nothing more than fiat currency, meaning they have value because a government says they are valuable—not because of any inherent scarcity or natural value.

Gold has inherent and natural value based on the market, while dollar bills rely solely on the faith of the users and government manipulation to maintain their value.

DIRTY DETAILS:

Only gold and silver are real money, just as they have been for thousands of years. These days, the "money" we carry around in our wallets isn't real money but rather a fiat currency made up out of thin air by the federal government and the Federal Reserve. Paper money is by definition a giant counterfeiting scam, but done legally by act of Congress. In 1971 President Richard Nixon took the United States (and thus the entire world) off the gold standard. This move turned our money into something called "fiat money."

A fiat monetary system means a system of money that isn't backed by anything except the faith of the people. Today this system is breaking down as the people, banks and governments holding the dollars are losing confidence in the reckless spending of bloated governments.

A question to ask is, do you think the United States government is going to suddenly, magically, balance its budget? Or, is it more likely that Congress and the White House will continue to drive multi-trillion-dollar deficits for years to come so politicians can stay in power?

If the politicians keep deficit spending, that means more borrowing. More borrowing means more printing of U.S. dollars. The more U.S. dollars in print, the less buying power each individual dollar will have. Simultaneously, as the dollar falls in value, gold and silver expand their purchasing power.

-4-

What makes gold and silver money? Why not cows, they're a commodity, right?

QUICK:

G old and silver have the five key things needed for anything to be money. These five things are:

- *Scarcity*
- *Durability*
- *Portability*
- *Fungibility*
- *Divisibility*

Silver and gold meet these five better than any other form of money or currency. Our current currency system—the U.S. dollar—meets the last four, but not the first one. Currency is not scarce in any way because the dollar, the yen, the euro, etc., are simply made up out of thin air by a central bank. There's nothing naturally scarce or valuable about them. Sounds a little like the Emperor's New Clothes fable.

For something to be useful money, it must serve these three purposes:

- *It must serve as a medium of exchange*
- *It must serve as a store of value*
- *It must be a unit of account*

35

DIRTY DETAILS:

The five keys for something to be useful as a form of money are:

Scarcity: *The item is naturally scarce. Things like gold, silver, diamonds, and uranium are all scarce. They have a naturally occurring supply and require labor and other resources to obtain them. Currency is not scarce because even though there is a finite amount in circulation at any given time, the central bank can double that amount at any moment. In fact, the Fed is doing just that, on a whim. The amount of currency it prints is arbitrary and completely artificial. The supply can be doubled or tripled in the blink of an eye simply by adding ink to paper and calling it money.*

Durability: *The item is naturally stable and maintains its physical structure and condition without being degraded over time. Gold, silver and salt are durable, but cattle and seashells would not be. Paper and plastic currencies wear out over time so they're not very durable. Currency is durable in digital form, unless the server the bank is using crashes or the digital money data gets corrupted.*

Portability: *The item is easy to transport. Gold and silver are easy to transport, as are dollars and diamonds. Real estate or livestock would be extremely difficult to transport.*

Divisibility: *The item must be able to be divided into equal reliable parts without losing the essence of it. Gold and silver are easily divisible down to microscopic amounts, without changing their essence. Although currency cannot be physically divided, governments have created smaller denominations (down to the penny in the U.S.) to allow for divisibility—and today's digital currency allows for infinite fractions of a penny as well. Cows, on the other hand, are very difficult to divide without losing the essence of the cow.*

What makes gold and silver money? Why not cows, they're a commodity, right?

Fungibility: *The item must be capable of mutual substitution with an identical item, meaning each individual unit of money can easily be swapped for another just like it. Any two nickels are the same and can be interchanged. Dollar bills have different serial numbers but are otherwise identical and worth the exact same as any other dollar bill. Precious metals are the same, as are individual shares of a stock. It doesn't matter which one you get; they're all the same. By contrast, every diamond is unique and must be priced individually. Thus, diamonds are not suitable as money. Every tract of land or head of cattle is likewise unique and not interchangeable.*

Precious metals, currency, oil, shares in a company are all fungible. Cows, tea, diamonds would not be.

The three keys for an item to serve as money are:

1. The item must serve as a medium of exchange. This means money is used as an intermediary for the exchange of goods and services as opposed to the direct exchange common in barter.

    In this way, you can avoid the inefficiencies in a barter system. You can trade your goods for currency and then hold on to that currency until you come across something else of equal value. Otherwise, you'd have to cross your fingers that you can find a person who has exactly what you want, when you want it, and needs exactly what you have, when you have it (something known as the "double coincidence of wants" problem). This type of barter typically slows economic trade to a grinding halt.

2. The item must serve as a store of value. A unit of money must be able to be saved and stored between

exchanges—and must maintain its same usefulness from the time it is gained to the time it is spent. The value, which means the purchasing power of the money, must remain stable over time. With the current system of fiat money, currency loses value over time due to inflation and is thus not serving its role as a store of value.

3. The item must be a unit of account. There must be a standard amount that is tied to the value of other goods. You can judge the relative value of an apple to a car by the amount of money (whether U.S. dollars, ounces of silver, etc.) it would take to purchase each. If a cow was being used as money, it would be impossible to identity the units of the cow to correspond to other goods. Currency is a very good example of standard units and works extremely well as a unit of account.

THE HISTORY OF GOLD AND SILVER:

Gold and silver, for whatever reason, rose into prominence in the free market environment and have been used as money for thousands of years. They're both naturally rare, which is why they've been sought for jewelry as adornment for millennia. They're extremely portable, able to be moved around with ease. They're also divisible, one ounce of gold or silver is indistinguishable from another anywhere else in the world, which makes them interchangeable.

Some other metals like tin and zinc are useful for industrial purposes, but they don't fit the requirements of money. The combination of scarcity, usefulness and human psychology all contribute to gold and silver's use as money.

Using precious metals as money isn't just a phase or fad like the Bit Coin rage was. Human beings have valued gold and silver for thousands of years. They've stood the test of time.

These two metals have a stronger and longer track record than anything else in history.

Warren Buffet hates precious metals right? That's what he says but he bought over one hundred million ounces of silver in 1998. Why did he do that?

Because at a deep and fundamental level, he understands the value of precious metals. He might try to convince himself that precious metals are a barbaric investment that doesn't pay dividends, but he didn't spend a half billion dollars on silver because he hates his money and wants to decrease his wealth. He knows what any savvy precious metals investor knows. Metals have inherent market-driven value today, just as they have for thousands of years.

Anyone can argue that gold and silver are just dumb metal and shouldn't be valuable. The market disagrees. Arguing with the market is generally a bad and expensive idea. The market has been saying gold and silver are money for thousands of years. The trend is your friend on this one.

DIAMONDS AND GEM STONES:

Precious stones are indeed scarce, portable and durable. But they are not in any way fungible or easy to identify. No two precious stones are alike and equal in value, as opposed to the equality of one ounce of gold compared to another. This alone eliminates stones from serving as a useful money option.

They're also not divisible. Breaking a diamond in half does not reduce its value exactly in half but rather reduces its worth dramatically. Plus, it's impossible to easily identity a stone's qualities without being an expert. Even the common man can recognize a silver eagle or gold eagle without trouble.

The value of diamonds, pearls, rubies and other precious stones is highly subjective. There's little to no consistency from one diamond to the next. They have value, but without being an expert or having a GIA (Gemological Institute of America) appraisal, the lay person would have no ideas of the precise or even ballpark value of the stone.

In this way, art is very like gem stones. Each piece is unique, and the value is extremely subjective, totally based on opinions. Both can be rare, beautiful and super valuable, but how—without being a trained and certified expert—can you tell the value of one piece compared to the next? In addition, most art lacks portability, divisibility and fungibility, making it useless as money.

-5-

What's the historical gold/silver ratio?

QUICK:

Historically the ratio has been in the range of 12:1 to 14:1. This ratio of value was set by the government and does not reflect the relative scarcity or availability of each metal.

DIRTY DETAILS:

The value ratio between an ounce of silver and an ounce of gold was set by government decree. A common misconception is that the ratio was a natural ratio that simply existed in nature.

Not so. The ratio was established based on a "best guess" about the relative scarcity of gold and silver (and not a particularly accurate one). Local governments would literally decree that a certain number of silver coins would be worth one gold coin.

These laws were determined by guessing how much more silver was available compared to gold. Lawmakers thought there was perhaps 12 times as much silver as gold, so they'd issue the official value ratio based on that assumption.

Today we have a better idea of what the real ratio is—and how terrible that old guess was. Instead of the ratio being 12 to 1, it's estimated to be 1 to 4. Yes, that's right, the current estimate of readily available gold on the surface of the earth is about four times *greater* than silver. Said another way, **silver is scarcer than gold**, four times scarcer. This makes silver insanely undervalued.

-6-

What's the difference between bullion, numismatics, coins and bars?

QUICK:

B ullion is essentially raw gold or silver in a coin or bar form. As you would expect, coins are usually circular and bars are rectangular. Otherwise, there is very little difference. Bars oftentimes have serial numbers stamped into the metal from the mint that produced them. The price you pay for bullion is very close to the spot price.

Numismatics, on the other hand, are collectible coins. With numismatics, you pay a premium for the collectible value of the coin. Since the collectible value has more to do with nostalgia than the value of the gold itself, it's highly subjective and much harder to evaluate the market value.

DIRTY DETAILS:

Bullion is a term that describes a common metal coin or bar. The value is derived almost completely from the actual gold or silver content, *i.e.*, the metal's value. Common bullion items are American Eagles, Canadian Maples, Swiss Bars and Johnson Matthey bars. These items are valued at the spot price, plus a small premium for production at the mint and, most likely, a dealer markup.

A key to bullion is that a one-ounce bar has almost an identical value as any other one-ounce coin or bar, even if they were minted at different places in different countries. This is because their value is tied almost entirely to the amount of gold in them. One ounce is one ounce, period.

Many unscrupulous dealers advertise bullion to the public and then try to talk the customer into buying rare, Proof and/ or Graded Coins (indicated so with a Mint State MS60-70 ranking) instead.

The foundation of any savvy investor's portfolio is bullion, preferably a well-known bullion such as American Eagles or Canadian Maple Leafs. Other bullion options like Austrian Philharmonics, South African Krugerrands, Australian Kangaroos and Swiss Pamp Bars are also superb. And unlike collectable coins, they don't require you to become a coin expert before you purchase them.

Bottom line, stick with the basics. When a dealer tells you their most popular product is a rare European gold coin or some other rare thing, they may be telling the truth, but the part they're leaving out is that their sales people make giant commissions on those items. No wonder they're a best-selling product if the seller is motivated by that huge commission! But that doesn't help the buyer at all. These dealers typically tell you to expect to hold these rare coins for three to seven years for appreciation. That's nonsense! It's only good for the dealer!

Numismatics, or collectable coins, typically carry a high premium above the spot or melt value of the coin. Unethical dealers often promote numismatic coins because of the arbitrary and subjective premium they can charge. The premium can easily be 20% to 100% over the metal value, and it often has more to do with the story behind the coin rather than the market value. (Which would you rather have, a precious metal or a precious story?)

These types of collectable coins are much harder to determine the market value of. And when it comes time to sell them, most dealers will only pay you for the gold or silver content. They're only interested in the weight of the coin, not the story behind it.

This is called the **melt value**. The melt value is the value of the actual gold or silver in the coin. Dealers know they can melt a coin and recover a certain amount of money based on that alone. The shape, engravings, imprints, etc., are unimportant. This is often the easiest way to value a coin and what many dealers will do when you try to sell them a collectible coin.

Rare coins are hard to sell for their sexy high value because of their very nature of being rare. The owner must find one of the few other people in the world who are interested in the coin's collectable value as opposed to its metal content. Bullion, on the other hand, is fungible and easy to sell anytime, anywhere.

EBay is a useful place to sell rare or collectible coins because the entire worldwide market of buyers is available to you. If you're going to sell a rare coin, I recommend first sending it to NGC to be graded and encapsulated with a serial number. This will provide proof of authenticity and condition before you put it up for sale on EBay or elsewhere.

As mentioned earlier, many shady brokers prefer selling the collectible coins and pushing them onto unsuspecting customers, often using emotionally charged stories to pitch the deal. The only party benefitting in these deals is the dealer.

One exception is the gold Double Eagle pre-1933 coins that were used as money before President Roosevelt made it illegal for American citizens to use gold or hold gold.

If you like collectible coins but don't want to worry about getting scammed by a bad dealer into buying bum coins, you'd be getting a fair deal on these old gold coins if you're paying 3% to 5% over melt (or spot) value.

In other words, you'd be buying a collectible but wouldn't be paying a significant premium for the "collectible portion." Almost all your money would be going for the actual gold content.

My favorite dealer in the collectible coin world is Marc Watts at Gaithersburg Coin Exchange. He's the most knowledgeable and honest dealer I've ever met, and he would be a great resource if you're interested in becoming a collector.

-7-

What's the difference between physical gold and paper gold?

"I heard I can buy a gold mutual fund and I don't have to worry about holding gold. Is this true?"

QUICK:

Paper gold is essentially a mutual fund for gold that was set up by Wall Street for that industry to make money by selling gold without losing control of their clients' money. In theory, paper gold is supposed to match the spot price of physical gold, and the fund should theoretically have the same amount of actual physical gold in reserves backing up the paper gold shares you're buying. This has never been proven or validated to be the truth. The discrepancy between the paper price and the spot price of gold is an indication that this Wall Street product is all smoke and mirrors, not real or genuine.

Buying paper gold is essentially owning a piece of paper that may or may not represent actual physical gold. On the other hand, physical gold you hold in your hand cannot be manipulated by Wall Street or anyone else.

I highly recommend only buying physical gold and silver if your objective is to hedge your wealth. Paper gold won't do it because it's tied to the same Wall Street system as the rest of the currency and paper markets, such as stocks and bonds. You run the risk of shell games and counter-party risk, which we'll discuss later. The paper gold strategy may seem easier, but it's a house of cards waiting to collapse.

DIRTY DETAILS:

The only safe gold and silver is real gold and silver that is physically in your possession or held by a dealer you trust. ETFs (Exchange Traded Funds) like paper gold and paper silver simply can't match the real thing.

These financial instruments are creations from the same maestros on Wall Street that created subprime mortgages and bilked the U.S. taxpayers out of trillions in bailout money. There is widespread belief in the precious metals arena that the ETFs do not have the gold they claim on their balance sheets to back up all the "gold shares" they're selling.

If you're buying 10 ounces of gold using an ETF, the vault may only have five or three or one ounce for those 10 ounces of paper gold they're selling. It's entirely possible that they may have no physical gold at all, just paper commitments for future delivery using the futures markets.

There's simply no way for you to know for sure. There's no audit to verify how much gold and silver are backing up the paper assets you're buying. EFTs are primarily for traders, not investors who want to preserve wealth.

Traders vs. Investors: The difference between a trader and an investor is primarily time and technique. A trader buys and sells quickly, rarely holding an asset long. (He may only hold it for minutes, hours or days.) He usually trades based on short-term, technical things like market panic or bliss, technical tops or bottoms, events in the news, etc. An investor buys something based on fundamentals and value, usually with intent to hold the asset for longer periods of time, years or decades.

The problem with paper gold is that this "thing" was made up by Wall Street bankers to serve them. As gold and silver became more popular in the early 2000s, the financial industry saw more and more money being pulled out of their control and invested into gold and silver. This movement presented a problem for them because they don't get to charge management or maintenance fees on money once it's left their firm. They also don't get to charge commissions on the transaction a client makes buying physical metals.

Wall Street's answer to this problem was to create pretend gold and silver, a product they could sell and represent as precious metals while maintaining their ability to charge commissions and management fees. These brokers sell the ETF shares by pitching them to clients who want the diversity of gold and silver without having to deal with holding the physical metal. They convince their clients that the ETF is the same as physical gold without the hassle of dealing with it physically.

Theoretically, you own rights to the gold. But if you look at the actual documentation for the ETFs, you'll find none of them allow you to exchange your "shares" for actual physical gold if you wanted it.

More importantly, none of them guarantee they have actual physical gold corresponding to the shares they're selling.

These paper gold funds are a shell game. In fact, there's speculation that there may be as much as 50 times more paper silver and paper gold than the actual silver or gold that's supposed to be backing it up all the shares being traded.

Basically, this means the whole paper gold and silver investment is a scam. The reason a full and transparent audit has not been—and never will be—made available for the public to view is because it would expose these funds to be a con job by the financial industry.

See Chapter 10 to read more about counterparty risk.

Bottom line, it doesn't make any sense to hold any of your wealth in paper gold or paper silver, unless you're a trader using the paper shares to buy and sell very quickly. The only real way for an investor to hedge in gold and silver over the long term is to own real physical gold and silver.

Remember, if you can't touch it, you don't own it!

-8-

Is buying gold and silver private? What gets reported to the government?

QUICK:

Yes, very private. Buying gold and silver is one of the most private investments possible. Dealers do not share any information with the government when a customer buys gold or silver unless the customer uses more than $10,000 in cash.

Whatever you buy is between you and the dealer.

When you sell to a dealer, in most cases the transaction is anonymous with a few exceptions seen below.

DIRTY DETAILS:

Gold and silver is highly private, primarily because you have total control of it. You physically possess it, and you can use it for whatever you'd like without the government having any ability to track it.

When you buy it, you and the dealer are the only ones who know that you have it. Once you have it, nobody other than you knows where you have it or even if you continue to own it. However, the Patriot Act requires a dealer to disclose any transaction involving $10,000 or more of cash in a single day.

When you're selling precious metals, the dealer isn't required to report anything unless the seller exceeds specific quantities of specific gold or silver items, in which case the dealer must file a 1099B with the IRS.

The 1099B forms are like other 1099 forms taxpayers commonly receive; the "B" means they have been issued by a business other than a financial entity.

Any sale of more than 25 ounces from a private party to a dealer involving one ounce Gold Maple Leafs, one ounce Krugerrands, or one ounce Mexican Onzas triggers a 1099B.

There are **no** reporting requirements for American Gold Eagles so you could sell 100 or 1,000 Gold Eagles to a dealer and the transaction would be private.

There are **no** reporting requirements for fractional gold coins.

There are no reporting requirements for any sale of American Silver Eagles, privately minted silver one ounce rounds and 100-ounce silver bars.

Selling bars and rounds over 1,000 ounces to a dealer does trigger a 1099B report that the dealer will send to the IRS.

Selling other precious metal products is likely reportable, but the above items are the most common and typically the ones more investors will hold.

Selling collectible coins to a dealer, unless you receive over $10,000 in cash, is not reportable.

Many dealers use privacy concerns to scare customers into buying overpriced collectible coins, but many bullion coins are completely private and carry very low premiums compared to the collectibles.

The most private investment for an investor to make without reportable sales is gold and silver American Eagles.

Any profit or gain from a sale is your responsibility to disclose to the IRS on your tax returns.

CASH TRANSACTIONS:

The IRS and the Patriot Act have rules requiring all dealers to fill out a Currency Transaction Report (CTR), the same report filled out by banks for any transaction involving $10,000 or more in cash. If you sell more than $10,000 worth of coins to a dealer and ask for cash, they are required to ask for personal information from you, including your social security number, to submit it to the IRS. This requirement is only for transactions over $10,000 in cash.

If a transaction is anything less than $10,000, a dealer has no reporting requirements. The rule is per day. If you sold $5,000 worth of gold for cash in the morning and then sold $7,000 worth of silver for cash in the afternoon to the same dealer, that dealer is required to combine the transactions for the purpose of filing a report with the federal government.

These are the rules. Most of what you will likely do with precious metals is extremely private.

-9-

Why doesn't my financial advisor suggest gold and silver?

QUICK:

Financial advisors almost never earn commissions or fees when their clients buy precious metals. They're in business to earn a living by selling products, so—as you would expect—they generally stick with the products they make money from selling. In addition, most financial advisors have a specific knowledge base that revolves around their own products.

Most self-described financial advisors have a narrow scope of expertise comprised of paper products like stock, bonds, mutual funds, annuities and life insurance. They simply lack expertise in precious metals and commodities. Without expertise in those fields, they wouldn't know what to recommend even if they had a way to make a fee from suggesting them.

DIRTY DETAILS:

Financial advisers are paid based on commissions they earn for selling specific products offered by the firm they represent. They're also paid fees for assets you have them manage. For a financial advisor to suggest you buy gold and silver, they're literally suggesting you take your money from them and cancel the possibility of them being paid on managing your investments.

A smart and honest advisor looking out for you will put your interests above his, so this wouldn't be a problem. Sometimes you'll get lucky and find a financial advisor who understands the value of actual diversification using gold and silver.

The most common thing to hear from a financial advisor is the suggestion that a client might want to move 5% to 10% of their assets into gold and silver. The advisor often mistakenly tells their client to buy an ETF, *i.e.*, paper gold and silver, sincerely believing they're helping the client out with hedging.

Why would a financial advisor, who makes money on managing your funds, want you to buy an ETF instead of physical gold or silver? Because if you buy an ETF, your assets are still under their management, and they are still getting management fees. The name of the game with financial advisors is to have as much of your wealth under their management as possible. A few financial advisors, the really great ones, will team up with a great dealer. Then, the advisor can recommend the dealer to their clients to purchase physical gold and silver. This is true diversification.

Great financial advisors can be of tremendous help in sorting out the complex nature of financial markets and investments. Just keep in mind that advising you to invest in physical precious metals is not in alignment with an advisor's financial interest because they have no way to get paid when you do that.

-10-

Why is the value of physical gold and silver nearly impossible to manipulate?

QUICK:

Physical gold and silver you hold can't be manipulated unless you decide to melt it. It's stable and safe. The biggest advantage is that it doesn't have any type of counterparty risk, which stocks, bonds and cash all do.

Gold and silver react to market forces and inflationary and deflationary triggers—such as central banks printing currency— but the market, the rules and decisions of others can't destroy the inherent and natural value in these precious metals.

Stocks can be manipulated by management decisions, stock exchange rules, political decisions, etc. Bonds are directly tied to the market interest rates, which can be manipulated up or down at any time by central banks—which changes the value of your investments regardless of how sound the actual asset is.

Cash is manipulated and devalued every time a central bank prints more currency and expands the supply. Every time interest rates are lowered or bond buying programs like QE2 and QE3 are implemented, cash gets crushed.

DIRTY DETAILS:

Gold and silver are currently the best investment and wealth hedge compared to stocks, mutual funds, bonds and cash. In the first 10 years of the 21st century, gold surpassed all other asset classes, and not by a little. It simply crushed these other classes. Gold and silver are likely to be the leaders during the second decade as well. Common sense suggests gold and silver will be the best assets to hold during the inflationary actions that will be taken by the central banks worldwide during the 2010s. Stocks and equity markets will continue to have problems for two reasons. First, the baby boomers are retiring, which means they're pulling money out of their retirement accounts rather than putting it in. This difference is getting larger and larger every month as more retire. This widespread selling will put downward pressure on the entire equities market.

Second, the public is nervous about a repeat of 2008 and losing their wealth to another crash. Their patience is not nearly what it was when they were told to just hang on and wait it out. Those investors watched as 50% of their wealth disappeared from their stock accounts in a matter of months. The next time there's a crack in the system that leads to a panic, the likelihood is the bottom will fall out and we'll see an even bigger correction than in 2008.

DERIVATIVES:

According to Richard Duncan, noted World Bank economist and author of *The Corruption of Capitalism*, there are some $700 TRILLION worth of derivatives still in existence worldwide. These things have been called financial weapons of mass destruction.

Derivatives include a wide range of "assets" from a credit default swap or a mortgage to options and futures for everything from soybeans to interest rates. A lot of these derivatives are toxic—*i.e.*, worthless—and yet they're still held on banks' financial statements at full value. Eventually they'll be exposed for the worthless paper they are, and the losses will have to be absorbed by someone. When that happens, companies will fail, stock values will fall, and markets will be shaken. Just a 1% loss on those derivatives is $7 trillion. That's equal to nearly half the GDP of the United States in 2011!

BONDS:

Bonds are in a bubble right now and poised to collapse. Bond prices had been stable for decades, and people have generally trusted in them and used them to provide cash flow.

In the recent past, they even increased in value as interest rates were lowered. The problem today is that interest rates can't go any lower since they're at zero. They have only one place to go, and that is up. When rates go up, which is 100% certain, the price of previously issued bonds will decrease, collapsing that market.

The inverse relationship between interest rates and bond values is well known but not being talked about by the Federal Reserve or Wall Street, even though the policies of the Fed are setting bonds up to collapse in the coming years.

This collapse of the bond market is as obvious and certain as knowing gravity will pull you down if you jump out of a plane. To attract more capital for a hungry federal government, rates on treasuries and bonds will eventually have to rise. Foreign investors are getting increasingly nervous about holding American debt and are starting to cut back. They're moving to more secure assets like gold and silver. As they do, the government will need to attract new debt holders. Thus, the government will be forced to raise rates, and the bond market will collapse under its own weight.

REAL ESTATE:

Many experts, including Robert Schiller and Peter Schiff, predict residential real estate prices will continue to fall. In fact, they expect home values will not return to their 2008 nominal values until 2020 or beyond. The price of real estate is highly susceptible to interest rates and government policy.

Recent government programs temporarily spurred residential activity, but tough lending standards and the ending of some of these government programs caused activity to slow. As loan rates move up, the exact opposite will happen to prices. They are sure to fall. The American people are loaded up to their eyeballs in debt and simply cannot afford to pay higher mortgage payments. Since people cannot afford more, their payments must fall—and there's only two ways for that to happen: lower interest rates or lower house prices. It's far more likely to be prices that fall than interest rates, which are already historically low in the current 3% range.

Along with home prices, commercial property is on the verge of a collapse in many locations. During the go-go 2000s, the easy lending and constant lowering of interest rates pushed development to hysterical levels by speculators. Now there's a glut of space available and not being filled. More and more people are defaulting on their leases and vacating. The value of commercial buildings is directly related to revenue streams that landlords receive in the form of rent. As those streams dry up, so does the value of the building. Commercial real estate will get pummeled as this correction plays out.

COUNTERPARTY RISK:

Precious metals are one of the only assets that don't carry any type of risk originating or triggered by another party's actions or inactions.

Any asset or investment you own that can be impacted by the action of another party and lose value has counterparty risk.

CASH:

Cash is not safe. Holding wealth in the bank is dangerous. As of fall 2010, the FDIC has identified more than 100 at-risk banks that it put on its "problem list." When JP Morgan bought Bear Stearns, they were allowed by the Federal Reserve and FDIC to hide $400 BILLION worth of suspect assets and keep them off the balance sheet. Who's going to be responsible for the losses when those assets collapse?

Taxpayers and holders of U.S. dollars—the funny money that's being printed at the speed of light—are going to be hit with that responsibility. The FDIC only insures $100,000 per depositor. If you have $200,000 in a single bank, even if it's spread among different accounts, when the bank fails you would likely only end up with $100,000.

Fundamentally, counterparty risk means that you have an investment that relies on some other party to perform an act for you in order for you to receive your investment back or your return.

For example, if you've got an insurance policy, there is counterparty risk. The counterparty is the insurance company. If they go out of business and your house burns down, you may be out of luck. Whenever a risk will be indemnified by another party in the event of loss, you've got a counterparty risk.

My personal experience with Counterparty Risk and FRAUD

In 2011, the financial system saw a criminal example of counterparty risk when MF Global collapsed. This brokerage firm misplaced over a billion dollars of client money that was supposed to be in trust accounts, untouchable by the firm, by law! The CEO, Jon Corzine—a heavily connected former U.S. Senator, Governor of New Jersey and Goldman Sachs executive—swore under oath to Congress he had no idea where the money went.

The clients of MF Global, including me, had cash with them that we used to hedge short-term risks. We were always under the impression that those cash assets were safe and couldn't be lost (since they were required by law to be held in trust).

The suspicion by many is that Jon Corzine and the criminals at MF Global were using client money to illegally place risky trading bets on European debt. When the trades failed and the money vaporized, they had to file bankruptcy. This was a very real lesson in counterparty risk and how easily anyone can be hit by the actions of others who disregard the rules in the name of greed.

All the clients relied on the firm holding client money in a separate, secure, untouchable location and not playing games or using it illegally. This type of illegal activity is a clear form of counterparty risk.

Counterparty risk doesn't exist with gold and silver because you hold your own physical gold and silver. There's no other party involved. Nobody can do anything that's going to impact your

actual assets. You're holding it. It can't just go away or be stolen
by hackers. Gold doesn't make bad investment choices. Silver
will not file for bankruptcy, because it made a bad decision.
Gold and silver are only affected by the real market of supply
and demand.

PART II

Why now?

- INTRODUCTION -

Who is investing in gold and silver today, and why?

Some of the biggest names in finance, along with some of the largest institutions on earth, are today directing billions of dollars into physical gold and silver. George Soros has billion-dollar bets on gold. Fellow billionaire John Paulson has billions of dollars in his hedge fund invested in gold. Even the University of Texas endowment fund has more than a billion dollars in gold bullion as of 2012.

The most successful investor of our time, Warren Buffett, bought over a hundred million ounces of silver in 1998.

Why are these very smart financial titans buying gold and silver? They know how valuable it is, how valuable it has been for thousands of years, and the likely direction it's headed.

The next section will shed light on why these individuals and central banks around the world are loading up on gold and silver—and why you should, too.

-11-

What is the bigger concern: inflation or deflation? What happens with gold and silver in either environment?

QUICK:

An inflationary environment (such as when currency is losing value from massive printing) drives the cost of all commodities higher. As a direct result, it also pushes investors toward the certainty of gold and silver.

In a deflationary period when commodities are losing value, gold and silver continue to maintain and oftentimes gain additional purchasing power because of their stability and reliability compared to other assets that are deflating. Notice I said, "purchasing power," not price. This is the most important consideration. Whether gold is at $500 per ounce or $5,000 per ounce, the question is what will that ounce of gold buy? This is the purchasing power, and it typically goes up for gold and silver during a deflationary period.

Gold and silver have a unique role in the market, as they are both money and a commodity. They have purchasing power, but they are also purchased with currency, so they respond to both markets.

DIRTY DETAILS:

The inflation/deflation argument is almost a moot point, because regardless of whether we have a high inflation or hyperinflation or a deflationary environment, the purchasing power of precious metals is almost certain to rise.

The reason for this is more about psychology. When people feel uncertain about their future due to war, strife or political chaos, they move assets to a place that is reliable and safe.

For most of the previous century, this safe harbor was U.S. dollars and treasuries. As the dollar and all currencies lose purchasing power in today's economy and treasuries are driven to zero interest, more and more investors are turning to the historical safety of precious metals.

When the economy and the world seem stable, including currencies, gold and silver are less interesting and tend to sit idly by without much change in purchasing power because people aren't worried.

In an inflationary environment, the dollar, the yen and the euro all lose value as more and more are printed. Meanwhile, gold and silver rise in value and purchasing power.

Even though Ben Bernanke and Tim Geithner repeatedly lie to Congress and the public by claiming they have inflation under control, their statements don't make it true.

Contrary to what they try to convince the public, the Federal Reserve and the U.S. Treasury Department are fully responsible for causing today's inflation. The cost of goods and services is rising in terms of dollars, but in terms of gold the prices of those same goods and services are stable or falling. Gold and silver now provide far more purchasing power than they did 10 years ago. Compared to real money, *i.e.*, gold, the value of the dollar has shrunk a mindboggling 80% in less than 10 years. In 2001, $1,000 bought about four ounces of gold. Today that same $1,000 will buy about half of an ounce. Experts predict that $1,000 will buy less than a fourth of an ounce in three to five years.

If the dollar loses 10% of its value, gold and silver aren't necessarily going to go up 10%. Likely, they will rise even further than that due to the emotion of the market. Fear and greed drive markets to irrational levels until the market corrects. In an inflationary environment, gold and silver are a great choice.

In a deflationary environment, people are scared and they tend to turn to assets that are stable. Gold and silver tend to be stable. Gold and silver are going to maintain a strong purchasing power as the price of commodities collapses in terms of currency. Deflation can be frightening when it happens quickly because people freeze into thinking falling prices will continue so they shouldn't do anything today. Slow and gradual deflation is fantastic for consumers. One only need look at the falling price of technology for tons of examples, from cell phones to computers, to realize how beneficial it is and how it drives wealth to higher levels in society.

It doesn't really matter whether we have an inflationary or deflationary environment. Either is going to result in gold and silver becoming more valuable, either in terms both price and purchasing power (in an inflationary environment) or in terms of purchasing power alone (in a deflationary environment).

-12-

Isn't the dollar backed by gold?

QUICK:

President Nixon "closed the gold window" in 1971. Prior to that, U.S. dollars (and every other currency linked to the U.S. dollar) were backed by gold. After Nixon pulled the plug, the dollar became totally fiat, meaning it was backed by nothing.

DIRTY DETAILS:

The dollar was backed by gold until 1971. In the 1960s, French President Charles de Gaulle saw the United States spending on the Great Society and the Vietnam War and started getting a little bit leery of the U.S. government spending all this cash. In large part his actions led to Nixon severing the gold standard.

With the dollar backed by gold, foreign governments with dollars could, at any point, send their dollars to the U.S. and exchange them for physical gold. As governments like France saw the U.S. spending outlandish amounts of money, they got nervous it was spending more than it held in gold reserves.

President de Gaulle acted to protect France from the wild spending of the United States. France started trading its dollars for gold and pushed the U.S. to the brink.

By 1971 the draining of gold was unsustainable. Either the U.S. had to slow its spending or sever the link between gold and the dollar. Nixon knew the country was running out of gold because of France and the system would eventually collapse. Thus, Nixon chose to preserve spending and closed the gold window, ending the gold standard with one quick swipe of the pen.

In the 40+ years since, the world has been on a fiat currency system. This means there is nothing backing the dollar, yen, euro, etc., except the faith of the people using the stuff.

The monetary system is overdue for a major correction after four decades of the current fiat system. It's likely to happen soon and abruptly. Historically the monetary system changes every 30 to 40 years. The last one was in 1971, of course. Before that, it was in 1944 with the Brenton Woods Accord, where all the currencies of the world were pegged to the U.S. dollar. (At that point, the U.S. dollar was still pegged to gold.) Prior to that, the last change was in 1913 with the introduction of the Federal Reserve.

Now, the likelihood is that we're going to see some sort of gold-backed currency again. It's unlikely to be the dollar (at least not a first), simply because doing so would restrain federal spending. It's more likely to be a currency from a country with a positive trade surplus like China and/or one that has an abundance of natural resources like Australia or Canada. The country adopting some type of gold standard first is likely to do a partially backed gold currency, which means every dollar or equivalent would be backed by, say, $0.25 worth of gold. This would be a fractional system, a 10% backing of the currency with gold. Whichever country does this first will transform their currency into the global leader of stability, precisely as the U.S. dollar was for nearly a century.

HISTORICAL PERSPECTIVE:

Gold and silver started off as a commodity money. This means the commodity is used as money. In this case, gold and silver coins were used as money and exchanged directly for goods and services.

The next evolution was a receipt system where the commodity was put into a depository or bank and the owner received a receipt. People started trading the receipts because it was easier than carrying around the metals. The receipts were portable and 100% backed by gold and silver, something real and tangible.

The receipts were treated as money and could be freely exchanged for the actual gold or silver at any time. The certificates were strictly representative of the actual gold and silver supply, so every certificate was backed by an actual commodity.

That was the nature of the banking system until the banks started playing games with pure one-to-one backing and, out of pure greed, created fractional reserve lending. The bankers realized people weren't coming back to get the gold and silver, but instead were just trading the certificates or receipts. The bankers realized they could print more certificates and loan them out, charge interest, and make more profits based on something they created out of thin air.

This type of plan would work unless people panicked and wanted their gold back. If the bankers printed twice as many receipts as they had gold for and all the receipt holders demanded gold for their receipts at the same time, the bank would fail.

This is where the confidence and faith of the people becomes critical. If the people with the paper receipts believe in and trust the banks, they'll keep the currency. If they believe the banks are playing games and ripping them off, they'll revert to the real money they trust: gold and silver.

The system of issuing more receipts or currency than the bank has the reserves to cover is called fractional reserve lending, and it's rampant all over the planet today. The difference today is that the actual gold backing the receipts has been eliminated from the equation. The banks now have deposits of currency that they lend out, but they lend multiples of what they have on deposit. They lend "money" out to people that is made up out of thin air. For more on this, please pick up a copy of G. Edward Griffin's book *The Creature from Jekyll Island*.

During the most recent financial crisis, fractional reserve lending was as high as 42 to 1. That means the banks lent out 42 times as much currency as they had in reserve. In some cases, the reserve went to zero so the bank didn't have to have any type of reserve at all. The banks just created money and lent it. They made profits from interest charged on loans of money they didn't even have. That's essentially what you have in your bank account, made-up cash that doesn't exist. There is nothing backing it.

This can seem a little crazy, and it is! That's why gold and silver—physical gold and silver—are so fascinating and so important, because they're real and can't be manipulated by anything like the fractional reserve system.

The reason central bankers and banks in general don't like gold and silver is because it's impossible to play games and make up money if the money is gold and silver. The banks lose their power to scam the populace.

-13-

If the dollar fails, are we going back to the gold standard?

QUICK:

The United States government and certain members of Congress, such as Ron Paul, are talking more and more about returning to some sort of gold standard before the dollar completely fails. Many other governments such as China and Russia are stockpiling gold reserves and are likely to announce the establishment of some sort of partial gold-backed currency. Some type of gold-backed currency is coming, even if it's not the dollar. When this happens, those with gold will see incredible growth in their wealth as the gold supply is once again tied to all the currency in circulation and gold is revalued accordingly.

DIRTY DETAILS:

If the United States went back to a gold standard, the new gold-backed dollar would have to account for all the fiat currency now in circulation. This type of accounting has been done numerous times throughout history and made those with precious metals very wealthy because they held real assets vs. the funny-money that had been created out of thin air.

In a situation where gold backed all the U.S. currency now in circulation, the price of gold would need find a price level in the range between $15,000 and $25,000 per ounce to account for current amount of currency that's been printed by the Federal Reserve.

The Federal Reserve has printed printing close to one hundred billion dollars a month for half a decade, further eroding the dollar and pushing the value of gold higher and higher. The more currency that is printed before the eventual accounting of dollars, the greater the value of gold will need to be—reaching far above the $15,000 to $25,000 range.

-14-

What happens when a currency gets devalued?

QUICK:

You need more cash to buy the same goods. Let's say Tuesday night you can buy a loaf of bread for $2, and then the currency gets devalued by the government at midnight. When you wake up in the morning, the loaf of bread hasn't changed, but now it costs $4 or more for the loaf. You just lost half of your purchasing power overnight.

DIRTY DETAILS:

When a currency gets devalued, one of several events usually triggers the devaluation. One event is when a new currency is taking the place of an old one, and people holding the old currency find their purchasing power falling rapidly. This happened in 1994 in Mexico. People woke up one day and had effectively lost the majority of the purchasing power their pesos had the night before.

Another form of devaluation is when additional fiat currency is printed, or the government changes how the money is valued. Whenever a central bank announces a stimulus like the Federal Reserve and other central banks have been doing since 2008, they are all devaluing their respective currencies by printing more currency to compete with the currency already in existence.

An explicit devaluation happened in the United States when the conversion rate of dollars to gold went from $20.67 per ounce to $35 per ounce on January 31, 1934. Overnight anyone holding dollars lost almost half of their purchasing power.

Said another way, one day your $20 bill got you an ounce of gold, and the next day your $20 bill got you 0.6 ounces of gold. That's a devaluation of currency.

Today the currency in your bank account or in your wallet is being devalued by the hidden tax called inflation. Every time the Federal Reserve announces a stimulus or a quantitative easing program, you're being hurt. They're printing more currency into existence, devaluing the dollars already out there, including those in your bank account.

Every time they do this, the newly created dollars are chasing the same fixed amount of goods in existence. This means the goods in existence will rise in price to reach an equilibrium between the supply and demand given the increased supply of dollars. The goods didn't get any more valuable as they rose in price; instead, the dollar dropped in value and its purchasing power decreased.

-15-

Isn't it too late to buy gold and silver? Isn't the price already too high?

QUICK:

No, it's not too late to buy gold and silver. A more accurate question would be: "Is the dollar going to continue to lose value because of Congress's spending and the Federal Reserve's printing?" The answer is undeniably yes. Gold and silver remain highly undervalued. You want to buy things that are undervalued and sell things that are overvalued.

The "price" of gold and silver is less important than the purchasing power of gold and silver. If you had an ounce of gold 100 years ago, it was worth approximately $20. This would have purchased a suit, a pair of shoes and a nice dinner out. While the price of gold kept rising, its purchasing power held steady for decades (equal to a suit, shoes, and dinner) until the first decade of the 21st century. Since then, it's purchasing power has climbed considerably.

Today, $20 will barely get you an appetizer, but that same ounce of gold will get you a custom-tailored suit, a fine pair of shoes at Saks and a half-dozen fine meals. The purchasing power of gold has strengthened, while the power of the dollar has collapsed—and will continue to do so.

The key is to hold your wealth in something that doesn't deteriorate over time. Dollars deteriorate and become worth less and less. Gold and silver maintain their value and purchasing power in good times, and in times of uncertainty, they gain purchasing power at the same time currencies lose their power.

DIRTY DETAILS:

The "price" of gold and silver is relative, but relative to what? Or, to phrase the question in market terms, "W hat's the purchasing power of gold and silver?"

Whether gold is $1,500 or $15,000 per ounce doesn't really matter in and of itself. It only matters how gold is valued relative to other things—food, clothing, land, housing, etc. If gold is valued at $15,000 an ounce but the average house costs $10 million, then suddenly the price of gold doesn't seem very high. In fact, at those numbers, an ounce of gold would be highly undervalued. On the other hand, if gold was $100 an ounce but an average new car only cost $200, gold would be extremely overvalued.

The "price" of gold is not what is important. The important thing to know is the purchasing power of gold and silver. Measuring the value of gold and silver *only* in terms of dollars doesn't tell you anything.

KEY RATIOS:

Key ratios are discussed in the chapter on selling (Chapter 21). For example, the **silver/house ratio** of ounces of silver it takes to buy a house is a key indicator of true value and purchasing power. In 2017, it takes approximately 12,000 ounces of silver to buy a house in the United States. Just a few decades ago the normalized ratio required about 1,000 ounces to buy a house. The current ratio indicates that silver is massively undervalued compared to housing.

Another value ratio we like is the **Dow/Gold Ratio**. This ratio asks, "How much gold does it take to equal the Dow Jones Industrial Average?". For example, if the Dow was at 20,000 and gold was at $1,000 per ounce, then the ratio would be 20:1. If the ratio ever hit parity, ie. it was 1:1, that's an indication that gold may be overvalued and/or something terrible has happened with the Dow.

Determining whether gold and silver are undervalued or overvalued can't be done with something artificial that can be created out of thin air in unlimited quantities (like the U.S. dollar). The true value must be evaluated in terms of other things that can't be created out of thin air, such as housing, oil, bushels of wheat, etc.

Gold and silver today are extremely undervalued compared to other real things. Ultimately, this means it's still early and you have time to buy precious metals. So, long as currency continues to be printed, gold and silver will keep chasing the printing presses and continue to rise in terms of dollars and overall purchasing power.

I suspect the price levels we'll see with gold and silver over the next few years will be mindboggling and, unfortunately, wealth-destroying for most people who are holding dollars— except those who've had the foresight to protect their wealth with hard assets.

PART III

The How...

-16-

How do I Diversify my Investments?

QUICK:

Spread your wealth between asset classes. These aren't what most people think.

Asset classes are:

- paper assets (stocks, bonds, mutual funds, cash)
- real estate
- hard assets (gold, silver, commodities).

A mutual fund or other similar collective assets that are all in one class—*i.e.*, stocks in different industries or bonds in different areas—still place all your wealth in that one class. This is not diversification.

DIRTY DETAILS:

Diversifying your portfolio is more than buying stocks in different sectors. Wall Street sold everyone on the idea that owning mutual funds or a variety of mutual funds means we're diversified. The truth is, owning mutual funds, even multiple mutual funds, puts all your assets in one asset class: paper.

Diversification is owning different asset classes. Again, the asset classes are paper, real estate and commodities. Owning a business could also be a separate asset class. If you don't have a mix of these different classes, you aren't truly diversified.

Gold and silver can be owned in physical form, where you can hold it in your hands, or you can have something called paper gold and silver. One type of paper gold and silver is an ETF (Exchange Traded Fund). ETFs are essentially a mutual fund that's supposedly backed by a big bunker full of gold or silver.

You hold paper that is supposedly a type of receipt representing actual physical metal, except there's no guarantee and *you can't convert the paper into real gold or silver.* Notice I said, "paper." You are still holding onto paper and not the actual commodity.

If everything is invested in the stock market, it doesn't matter how many different stocks you have, the market direction determines your portfolio. If the market goes down in equities, your whole portfolio drops.

ETFs are much more heavily affected by the stock market and the spot price than physical gold and silver are. Wall Street continues to propagate a huge myth that you're well diversified if you have stocks in different industries or if you hold mutual funds. These assets are still just paper and all are affected by the global financial markets. If the stock market crashes, all of those "diversified" mutual funds will still simultaneously crash. By truly diversifying, you spread risk into different classes and sectors; plus, you can influence the values. You have no power or control over your assets if you own equities.

-17-

How much do I really need to know before investing in gold and silver?

QUICK:

You know enough by reading this book. You know that the economy has problems, that the dollar is falling in value, and that it's your responsibility to take care of your own financial future. No politician is going to save you, no matter how many claim they will. You are responsible for your own fortune. Relying on the government is a fool's game.

DIRTY DETAILS:

After reading this book, you should have a sense of why gold and silver are smart to hedge your wealth with. You should also know why now is a critical time to invest in them. The balance of the book gives you the "how to" information, *i.e.*, how to buy, how to hold, how to sell, etc.

This is enough to get started hedging with gold and silver.

Stocks and bonds are much trickier than gold and silver, but Wall Street has brainwashed the population to believe these paper assets are safer and better to invest in. Stocks require a lot of education to figure out what to buy, what a company's financials mean, the quality of management, trends in the equity market, and future profit expectations. With gold and silver, you just need to know how to purchase it, where to store it, how to insure it, and how to find a great dealer.

This book gives you everything you need to get started and to safely invest in gold and silver.

You have two options for precious metals. The first option will make you crazy and stress you out. You can watch the market every day and try to time everything perfectly based on day-to-day gyrations in the commodity world.

A better, sounder and peaceful option is to use gold and silver as a nest egg that will continue growing on average if you own it. (Yes, there will be times that the price dips, but the long-term history is clear: gold and silver continue to increase in value, especially as fiat currencies are mass printed).

-18-

How do I buy gold and silver? How do I pick a great dealer? What makes a great dealer? What's the best criteria for picking a world class dealer?

QUICK:

C all a trusted precious metal dealer and ask them to walk you through the process. If you don't know one, test out a couple of dealers with nearly perfect ratings on Amazon. com or eBay. Both Amazon and eBay have extremely strong protections for you when you buy, so they are among the safest options for getting started.

When you speak with a dealer, I suggest you stick with the basics. Ask for gold and silver one-ounce bars, or ask for gold and silver Eagles and Maples. Either are simple and sound bullion options.

DIRTY DETAILS:

You have a few different ways to buy gold and silver. When you're first starting out, you can find somebody on Amazon. com or eBay. These are great options if you don't know anyone and are starting from scratch. It's a great way to locate a dealer and see how they operate, how they communicate, and overall how they treat you.

Amazon and eBay have strong buyer protection systems. You're going to pay a premium using either of these, but in the beginning, I suggest using them until you're comfortable buying direct from a dealer you've built trust with.

EBay auctions can be great places to buy small amounts of silver, a coin or two at a time. I highly recommend buying from people with 99% to 100% positive feedback and a long-term track record of world class service. You can see this from the testimonials tied to any dealer on eBay.

Once you find a dealer you want to do business with, call them and ask them to walk you through the process. You'll likely tell them what you want and they'll give you a price you can lock the order in at. Once it's locked in, they'll be able to give you a confirmation number.

Most dealers (including me) give the clients a couple of options for paying. On small orders, we'll allow a check to be mailed, but on larger orders we generally require payment to be wired within 48 hours. Some dealers will ask for a credit card to keep on file that they'll charge if you fail to send a check or wire. This is a common practice for a first-time order from a new client.

Beware of a dealer who says, "Just send me money, and I'll let you know what the price is later." It can be very, very dangerous to do this with most dealers. Only after you've built a long-term relationship with a dealer would this type of transaction be even remotely safe.

Some dealers require a new client to send funds first and won't lock in a price for a new client until the funds arrive and clear. This is because they don't know how reliable you are and if you're going to send them a check in a week, a month, or ever.

How do I buy gold and silver?
How do I pick a great dealer? What makes a great dealer?
What's the best criteria for picking a world class dealer?

They don't want to lock in your price and then have the market take off or crash and be stuck.

You should make sure you're comfortable that the dealer will buy the products back that you're buying from them. Ask them what their buyback price is for the items. It should be approximately 4% to 6% less than your purchase price.

My favorite way to find a new dealer is by referral from someone I trust. Ask people you know (the financially savvy ones, not the dead broke ones). Ask them if they've done business with a great dealer.

When you first start a relationship with a dealer, it's important to test them. Start with a small transaction. Build a relationship and see how they operate. See if they do what they say they're going to do. Do they ship when they promise to? Do they give you something different from what you thought you were buying? What's their buyback policy for when you want to sell?

MY CRITERIA FOR PICKING A WORLD CLASS DEALER:

My favorite dealers are the one I've done business with and who I know will do exactly what they tell me they're going to do every time, without exception. The dealers I work with are looking out for me all the time; I trust they'll watch my back and will never, ever take advantage of me.

I know the dealers are making a fair profit from every transaction with me, and I have no problem with it. A great dealer makes a fair profit and provides you CERTAINTY about the transaction. The last thing you want to do with a great dealer is screw around with them on price when their margins are only a few percent anyway. You'll annoy them, and they'll stop taking your calls.

The most important part of your relationship with a dealer is reliability and honestly. My clients know we're not the cheapest option for their gold and silver. We might be 1% more than they can find from someone else, but they have no problem paying an extra penny for world class service, reliability, transparency and the protection we provide them. One percent is a small price to pay for complete confidence in your investment.

Don't get cheap on this—it will cost you a fortune!

Here's my check list and rules to use for any dealer you're considering.

NEW DEALER RULES:

- If you don't know anybody and no one you know can recommend anybody they've done business with, the Better Business Bureau is a great place to go. It's worth it to look at the complaints and the reviews. You really don't want to work with anyone who has lower than an "A" rating. The BBB is where consumers go when they have a problem with a company. If a company is doing something screwy or sketchy, they'll complain and you can read about the complaints. Most importantly, you can see how the company responds. Just because a company has a complaint doesn't mean you shouldn't do business with them, but if their response makes you nervous, think about how you'd feel if your money was involved. This is a good warning to steer clear.

- How old is the company? You can see this on the BBB website. Is it brand new or only a couple of years old? I like companies that have been around for years—and decades is even better. A lot of startups are forming because of the gold boom, but it's hard to tell if they're solid or will be "here today, gone tomorrow" when you

How do I buy gold and silver?
How do I pick a great dealer? What makes a great dealer?
What's the best criteria for picking a world class dealer?

really need them. When you're looking for a dealer, look for someone who's been in business for five to ten years or more. It helps if they've been in business for several decades and have some folks with grey hair who've been through a complete cycle.

- What's their buyback policy? Are they transparent or is it confusing? What happens when you want to sell? Is it fast and easy? You should specifically ask if they'll buy back the items you're buying from them. What's their spread? This means, what's the difference between what you're paying and what they'll pay you for the same thing. Dealers you see on television have very large spreads. You might buy something for $100 and the dealer would only offer you $70 or $80 if you wanted to sell it back.

  With our company, you'd likely see a spread of 4% or 5%. A very small spread is what you want. This means the item doesn't have to double in value for you to break even. You don't want to be underwater forever, waiting for something to get to a breakeven point.

  Another question is, how long does it take to get paid for items you want to sell? With us, you can have money as quickly as one day from the day you call us to sell anything. It's quick and very simple. Our process is laid out on our website and very transparent.

- Do they have a brand-new office building with lots of overhead? If yes, I suggest you run away. I say that because a new shiny building means huge overhead, and all that expense gets passed on to you, the customer. Those dealers typically have higher than necessary markups, and they tend to push high-premium collectable coins that you probably shouldn't be buying in the first place. That's how they pay for their swanky offices. I prefer online dealers or dealers who've been around for decades in an old brick buildings without mortgages. They tend to have a lot of my next requirement:

- Does someone in the company leadership have gray hair? If everyone is fresh out of college, you'd be wise to move on because you're most likely dealing with wildcatters who weren't around during the last cycle. They have no idea what it's like to be in a gold and silver boom/bust. And they're often trained only in selling to you rather than protecting your wealth with hedging strategies.

- Television commercials... Do they have any? If yes, RUN! I say to run because television commercials cost a ton. The money to pay for those ads comes from...yep, highly marked-up products! Television commercials = big markups!

- Are you a collector of relics or are you an investor wanting to hedge and diversify into commodities? If you're a diehard collector, then your local coin shop is the best place to go and poke around for old coins, hold them, and gaze into history. If you're an investor and want to diversify and hedge with gold and silver, you want a dealer who sells bullion, period.

Bullion is the best deal, the biggest bang for your buck, and you're not going to pay huge premiums that could take years to get back. See Chapter 6 about **Bullion** vs. **Numismatics** for more on this. In my experience, the big dealers like Goldline, American Bullion and all the other dealers you see on television sell bullion AND numismatics, but they will generally focus on selling high-margin, high-markup numismatics because their sales people make the most on them. They also must pay for all those expensive commercials!

If all this stuff checks out, look on eBay and Amazon to see if the dealer you're considering is doing business on those

How do I buy gold and silver?
How do I pick a great dealer? What makes a great dealer?
What's the best criteria for picking a world class dealer?

marketplaces. You can see what their customers are saying about them without any type of filter (like you might find on a company's own website). Businesses don't have the option to sanitize their testimonials on Amazon or eBay. They're real and authentic.

You can see our reviews on both Amazon and eBay by looking up My Gold Advisor.

THE TEST

I highly encourage you to test the dealer by doing a small trial purchase. Buy some silver Eagles or a gold Eagle or Maple Leaf. Spend a few hundred bucks buying a gold bullion coin or a roll of silver coins, and see how the transaction goes. Do you feel pressured? Did you get pushed to buy something you didn't want or don't really understand?

Then, call the dealer about three weeks later and tell him you'd like to sell the item you purchased back to him. See what happens. You'll learn a ton by going full circle, buying and selling from the same place. You'll learn what their actual spread is and what you're likely to experience during a larger transaction with the dealer.

Keep in mind that you're likely going to get less than you paid for the item (unless, of course, gold has gone up at least $80 an ounce or silver has gone up $2 an ounce during the quick three-week period between your purchase and your sale). This is normal, and the difference is called the spread.

When you buy the items, the dealer should be able to tell you what to expect when you want to sell. Then when you see them, you can see if the dealer was being straight with you. It will also give you total confidence and clarity about how the entire transaction looks—including how quickly you get paid, how your metals physically get to the dealer, etc. There's no better way to learn the truth than by doing something.

QUESTIONS TO ASK THE DEALER:

- What's the current price above spot?
- What's the total amount for the order?
- Will the dealer buy back the product he's trying to sell you and, if so, at what price? Scammers and rip-off artists will either not buy the products back or will buy them back for a giant discount. Solid dealers make a small spread (3% to 5%) and will be happy to buy anything back from you at any time.
- Ask yourself if the dealer is more focused on educating you or selling you on the reasons to buy now. Ask all of your questions and if you have any hesitancy or feel like you're being pushed into something you're not comfortable with, HANG UP!

The idea is to make sure you pick a dealer who's honest and reputable so you're not constantly worried about being ripped off.

PAYING FOR IT:

If you're buying anything with a credit card, it will be about 2.5% to 3% more than if you use cash, a check or wire. With cash, check or wire, you should expect to spend about 5% over the spot price on Gold Eagles and about 10% over spot on Silver Eagles. The more you buy, the better pricing you'll receive—and you'll likely get free shipping, etc. We offer complimentary FEDEX shipping on all orders over $1,000 and better pricing on quantities of five or more coins of any size.

How do I buy gold and silver?
How do I pick a great dealer? What makes a great dealer?
What's the best criteria for picking a world class dealer?

SPLITTING YOUR MONEY BETWEEN GOLD AND SILVER:

Silver is likely to be a better performer because it's more undervalued then gold. At the same time silver tends to be more volatile than gold. Therefore, the more aggressive you want to be, the higher percentage of your money you might want to put in silver. Silver will easily move 3% to 5% in a day while gold is more likely to have daily moves of 1% or 2%.

If you have the wits to stay calm during market volatility, you should consider a larger position in silver than gold. I prefer something like a 3:1 split: 75% silver and 25% gold. A lot of people split it 50-50, and it helps them feel more stable. Regardless, I think at least 50% of your metals portfolio should be in silver.

It's definitely a good idea to split between gold and silver instead of having everything in one or the other. This allows for a little more diversity within your portfolio. See Chapter 16 to learn more about diversifying your portfolio.

If you're nervous and any move in the market gives you heartburn, a larger portion should probably be in gold.

LIQUIDITY:

Liquidity or "being liquid" means your assets can be converted into cash quickly and easily.

For gold and silver liquidity means you can sell the coins or bars anywhere in the world at any time for a fair price. If they're liquid, you wouldn't have any problem trading them for the local currency. The opposite is true for collectible coins.

A bullion bar or coin is recognizable not only to any dealer but also to ordinary people. Anyone that knows anything about gold and silver would be able to recognize it. There's no mystery about what it is and no need to research its story. With bullion bars and coins, it's also easy to identity how much gold and silver are in them. Typically, the amount is stamped right into the gold (or silver).

This is different than paper gold (ETFs), stocks, bonds or real estate. All of those investments require a middleman in order to cash out. The market must close, the funds must be transferred, and paperwork may be required. With gold and silver, you can change them into any local currency nearly instantly. If you want to go to Paris for a surprise vacation and you have a gold Maple Leaf, you'd have no problem selling the coin to a local dealer for euros.

SELLING DURING A PANIC OR BUBBLE:

One of the most important reasons to have a relationship with a dealer that you know on a **first-name basis** is so you can convert your precious metals into cash or other assets quickly, at any time.

During panics or a bubble collapse, dealers and smelters are overwhelmed with people selling metals. The best dealers and brokers will have access to the wholesale market and be able to provide you with an avenue to sell your gold and silver anytime you want at current prices. If you don't establish a strong, personal relationship in advance—*before* you need it—you'll be in line with everyone else, way behind those who established these relationships.

At My Gold Advisor, we always take care of our private clients first, before the public. Our clients know they have access to us

How do I buy gold and silver?
How do I pick a great dealer? What makes a great dealer?
What's the best criteria for picking a world class dealer?

when they need us, and they know we're ready to serve and take care of them when they need us, not just when it's convenient to get to them. Once you're a client of ours, you take priority ahead of the public.

Gold and silver have always been money, will always have a market, and will always be convertible into other things like cash. Make sure you build a relationship with a dealer so you have access to the current market and are certain of your metals' liquidity whenever you need it.

FAIR PRICING:

If you're buying small quantities, *i.e.*, up to a few hundred-dollars' worth of coins at a time, eBay and Amazon are usually the best sources to buy at competitive prices. When you want to buy several thousand dollars' worth of metals or more, the most important thing is to make sure you're dealing with a dealer you trust, not just the best price.

A great way to cut to the chase with a dealer is to ask what they'll pay for items they're selling to you should you want to sell them back. A sound dealer will be able to instantly tell you what their buyback price is without any hesitation at all.

The more popular gold and silver get, the more often I run into offers to buy gold and silver at prices 1% or 2% less than what I pay from my favorite dealers. I don't bother going to the cheapest place because I have a relationship and a ton of trust with the companies I'm already working with. I'm very happy to pay that small extra premium knowing they'll take care of me and will always act with integrity in our transactions. Establish a relationship with a dealer you like and stick with them. Knowing you're working with a sound dealer is usually worth much more than the few pennies you might save from the wheeler-dealer of the week with cheap prices.

The markets are volatile enough that the last thing you want to worry about is whether your dealer is going to rip you off.

If you want very small quantities—like an ounce or two of silver—the best price you'll find is usually eBay auctions. You can usually go online and buy coins one or two at a time for close to the spot price. However, if you want to buy anything more than a few ounces of silver or anything larger than an ounce of gold, the best plan is to go to a dealer that either has a very old store or a virtual dealer like My Gold Advisor. These are the dealers who don't have an expensive lease or the high overhead of a big office and can offer you low-margin markups on your bullion.

You run into more fees and higher markups the more overhead a dealer has. You'll also run into dealers who are pushing numismatics (the high markup collectible coins) if they have the overhead.

One thing to keep in mind: there isn't a magic moment to buy or a month of the year that gold is always going to be cheaper than other months. Once you find a dealer you trust, if the dealer doesn't have a lot of overhead or added fees, you're likely getting a good deal.

Always ask a dealer how much they'd be willing to buy your coins back for when you're asking them about the purchase price. The difference between the bid and ask price is called the **spread**. The bid is what they'll pay you, and the ask is what they'll sell them to you for. Stick with dealers who have a 3% to 6% spread.

-19-

How is the spot price different from the actual value of physical gold and silver?

QUICK:

The spot price is a guide to help determine the value of physical coins and bars. Spot is the value of the metal on the futures exchange and is a part of the physical metal price. The real market is comprised of the spot price, plus the production cost (or minting expense), plus the dealer profit.

DIRTY DETAILS:

The spot price, or the price you see in the media for gold and silver, is different from the cost to buy coins and bars. However, the spot price is the basis to determine the price of them. Let's look at a couple examples.

SILVER EAGLES:

The most common silver bullion coin is the American Silver Eagle so we'll use this for our example on how pricing is determined. For this example, let's say the current spot price is $35. The production and minting costs average about $2.50 per coin, and the dealer profit is $.90 to $2 per coin, depending on the number of coins being purchased. In this case, we have $35 + $2.50 + $1.50. This means your price would be $39. This is the ask price.

(Side note: A common amount to buy from a dealer is a 20-coin roll. Buy less than 20 and you'll pay more per coin because it's time-consuming for a dealer to work with small or odd amounts.)

The price you can expect if you were to sell those coins to a dealer like My Gold Dealer would be spot plus about $1 to $1.50 per Silver Eagle. Therefore, you'd receive about $36 to $36.50. This would be the bid price.

GOLD EAGLES:

Gold Eagles are similar but have smaller margins in most cases. Let's say the spot price for gold is $1,800 per ounce. The mint and production premium is about 3.5% and a fair dealer markup is about 3% for one or two coins. (Larger amounts would generally result in a lower markup by the dealer.) Therefore, a fair price to pay would be $1,800 + $63 + $56, or $1,919 per coin.

The price you can expect to receive to sell gold Eagles to a dealer like My Gold Advisor would be the spot price plus 1% to 2% per Eagle, or $1,818 to $1,836.

EAGLES vs. COINS and BARS:

The reason we recommend Eagles instead of bars or coins is because of incredibly high liquidity they have. Gold and silver Eagles are easy to sell anywhere in the world very quickly. They're well known and trusted.

You'll pay a little bit more when you buy the Eagles than you would for a bar or coin, but you'll also get most of that premium back when you sell the Eagles to a dealer or another party.

104

Any well-known bullion is fine to purchase for your gold and silver portfolio. My personal preference is the Eagle and the Maple Leaf because of their worldwide recognition and acceptance compared to other, lesser known forms of bullion.

A great choice for you if you'd like a gold bar is the Suisse Pamp, which is very well known, very liquid, and has only a small markup. These are very popular with our clients.

SPOT:

The spot price is what major institutional buyers and bullion banks are paying on commodities exchanges around the world for all sorts of commodities including gold and silver. These trades are primarily futures contracts and do not involve physical delivery. The spot price is about the futures value. This is the value for delivery of gold or silver in the next 30 days.

When you see oil in the news for $92 a barrel, that's the spot price. This is the price for a barrel of oil that will be delivered in the next month.

Let's say it's September now, and we say, "Gold is at $1,690." That's the amount the market is saying gold is valued at for delivery in the middle of October.

The Chicago Mercantile Exchange, often called COMEX, is one example of a futures market. It deals in commodities like metals, agriculture, oil, etc.

BULLION:

Bullion is the term for a coin or a bar in an easily recognizable form and using the spot price as the basis for its cost to you. There are millions of bullion coins, which is why the premium on them is small and they can be purchased for only a small amount over the spot price.

BULLION VS. SPOT PRICE:

In general, the price you pay for bullion coins and bars is a mixture of the spot price, production cost and dealer markup. Gold bullion coins are generally 4% to 6% over the spot price. Silver bullion coins are generally 7% to 11% over spot, a bit higher because the mints charge a higher premium for production.

FRACTIONAL GOLD:

Other less liquid products like the fractional gold one tenth, one fourth, and one half ounce Gold Eagles carry higher premiums because of the costs associated with minting them.

FIGURING OUT YOUR GOLD AND SILVER VALUE TODAY:

Call your favorite dealer or look up the spot price on the internet. Multiply that times the number of ounces you own. This will provide a fairly good idea of how much your metals are worth.

At My Gold Advisor, you can add 1% to 5% to the spot price to figure out how much your stuff is worth since we pay more than any other dealer in most cases.

-20-

How do I store my gold and silver?

QUICK:

Gold and silver don't take up much room, but due to their value it's smart to secure them and keep the knowledge of their existence, private. My favorite way to store metals is in a safe at your house or a third party private vault.

Five hundred ounces of silver fits in an average shoebox. This is about $10,000 in 2017. Seven hundred ounces of gold fits in the same size shoe box and is worth about a million dollars in 2017.

DIRTY DETAILS:

There are a couple of different options for storing your gold and silver. You can store them at home, in a safety deposit box, or in a vault.

Most our clients keep their metals at home in a safe. I recommend bolting the safe to the floor and keeping the metals in the safe. It's best to put the safe somewhere inconspicuous, not in the middle of the living room.

Make sure the safe is fireproof so a house fire won't destroy all your assets. And make sure it is a difficult safe to open. Some safes out there are thick and sturdy, but easy to pick.

SPACE/SIZE:

A hundred thousand dollars' worth of gold bullion will fit in a normal-sized coffee cup. One million dollars' worth of gold would easily fit on a normal sized dinner plate. Silver takes up a bit more space. Twenty thousand dollars' worth (approximately 500 ounces) would fit in an average shoebox.

A medium-sized gun safe would hold all the silver and gold most people would ever have in their life.

If you don't want to hold it at home, you can put it in a safety deposit box at a bank—although we discourage it because safety deposit boxes are not FDIC insured. In an era of failing banks, the last thing I'd want is for my bank to fail and seal my box so I couldn't get access to my metals.

PRIVATE VAULTS:

Another option is a third party privately insured vault. Some vaults are large institutions that hold your metals for a monthly fee based on value. Others like My Gold Advisor are specialized boutiques with unique services.

My Gold Advisor offers storage services with an instant cash and wire option. With this option, a client can call our vault and sell any portion of their metals with the proceeds wired to them the same day.

They can also have any part of their portfolio shipped by FEDEX to any location in the world by simply placing a phone call.

These services provide peace of mind to clients that their metals are protected while still ensuring they have instant liquidity at any time and any place. The last thing you want is to have your metals stuck in a vault when you need cash for something.

Some vaults require a week to ship your metals to a dealer to be sold and then you could be looking at another week to get a check from the sale.

My Gold Advisor offers a complete spectrum of in-house precious metals services for all clients, whether they purchased their metals from us or from anyone else. Access and liquidity are available with a quick call.

One warning: if you ever store precious metals in a vault, we highly encourage you to choose **allocated storage**. This means the metal you're storing is specifically earmarked as yours and you can get access to it anytime you'd like.

With unallocated storage, your metals may be mixed with other client's metals.

The first choice for storage is at home in your own safe, but it's totally a personal choice. As far as how much space it takes, you can see that it doesn't take much space.

INSURANCE:

We encourage you to keep knowledge of your metals to as few people as possible. Keep it private. It's also a good idea to get your gold and silver insured. If you need access to a third-party insurance company specializing in high-value items like this, feel free to contact me and I'll share some of our contacts. Most homeowners and renters policies do not offer coverage above $5,000.

-21-

How do I sell my gold and silver?

QUICK:

C all your favorite dealer! Wherever you are in the world, there will be dealers willing to buy your gold and silver.

If you're in the United States, you'll generally do well by selling to a low overhead dealer that does a large volume of bullion business. These types of dealers have low margins, meaning you'll get the most for your bullion. My Gold Advisor is one such dealer.

DIRTY DETAILS:

When you want to sell your gold or silver, give your favorite dealer a call and tell him what you want to sell. If you don't have a relationship with a dealer, your best bet is to go into a local coin dealer and bring the items you're ready to sell. They can cut you a check right on the spot.

If you have a relationship with a dealer, like the one you bought the items from, you can usually get a quote over the phone on the stuff you want to sell. If you're agreeable, the dealer will lock in the price.

Once you have a price lock, write the confirmation number down and package your stuff up to send to the dealer. Don't forget to include your address and the confirmation code. Some dealers like My Gold Advisor will wire payment directly to you as soon as they receive your package. We do this free of charge for our clients.

The most important thing is to make sure you trust the dealer you're selling to. Make sure they have a high BBB ranking, no less than an "A." Also make sure you can get them on the phone whenever you need to.

Remember, you'll be shipping your package to them and you must trust they're going to send you the money as promised. It's critical that you trust them and they're reliable.

WHEN DO I SELL?

Sell when you need cash to buy something you need or when gold and silver are overpriced. You'll have a good idea when gold and silver are overpriced when certain key ratios are met.

Just because gold and silver moves up 5% this week doesn't necessarily mean it's a great time to sell. The best time to sell your gold or silver is when you have another, better use for your money.

KEY RATIOS:

We watch ratios. These ratios give us an indication of when gold and/or silver is going from undervalued to overvalued. These ratios help us decide when we might want to switch some of our portfolio into another asset class.

GOLD TO SILVER RATIO:

One key ratio we watch is the ratio between gold and silver. The ratio of gold to silver in 2017 is about 50:1, which means it takes 50 ounces of silver to buy one ounce of gold. When this drops to 12:1 or 15:1, we'd consider selling some of our silver and converting it into gold.

At a ratio of 50:1, you can buy a lot more silver than gold today. As the ratio shrinks from 50:1 down to 15:1, silver is becoming more closely linked to gold and it requires less silver to get the same amount of gold.

When it takes less silver to buy an ounce of gold (like 12 ounces of silver to one ounce of gold), then gold is heading "lower" and silver is heading "higher."

During periods of history when gold and silver served as the foundation of the world's economy, this ratio was typically between 14 and 16. Whenever we suffer a global monetary crisis… (like today)…whenever people begin to fear that the world's paper currency system will break down… the price of silver tends to rise far more than gold.

We expect this ratio to eventually reach the mid-teens again because the ongoing massive global inflation will inevitably lead to a collapse of the dollar standard and to the return of gold-backed currencies.

This implies a massive increase in the price of silver. It's the best commodity to own to hedge against a big monetary inflation, which is exactly what's going on around the world.

MEDIAN HOUSE TO SILVER RATIO:

When you look at the median house price in the United States compared to silver in 2017, it takes about 5,000 ounces of silver to buy a median-priced house. When the ratio gets closer to 500:1, meaning 500 ounces of silver will buy a median-priced house, this would be an indicator that it may be time to switch from silver into residential real estate.

When silver can buy that much house, it would indicate prices of residential real estate have come down to a point where silver may be getting overpriced and/or housing is undervalued.

We want to buy things that are undervalued ("low") and sell things that are overvalued ("high").

DOW TO GOLD RATIO:

Another ratio we watch is the Dow/Gold Ratio. This is the ratio of the number of ounces of gold it takes to equal the Dow Jones Industrial Average. The Dow has been around 22,000 in late 2017. Gold is around $1,300 per ounce, so the ratio is about 17:1. It takes seventeen ounces of gold to match the Dow. When the ratio is closer to 1:1 or even 2:1, we might consider selling some gold and buying equities.

GETTING THE MOST WHEN YOU SELL:

Use a dealer you know, trust and respect—and preferably one you've done business with in the past. Never go to a *Cash4Gold* or other *We Buy Gold*-type of business in your local strip mall.

One of the funniest parts of the gold and silver bull market we're in is all the "cash for gold" stores popping up. It's funny because they tend to be an empty room in a strip mall with a window sign saying, "We Buy Gold!" Inside you'll find a counter, likely behind a bulletproof window.

There's a reason those things are popping up everywhere. These businesses generate huge margins and huge profits for the dealers. They do this by ripping off the consumer.

Let's say you bring a pile of your old jewelry into one of these stores and that jewelry contains four ounces of gold. At a spot price of $2,000 an ounce, the melted value of your gold is $8,000. In most cases, these businesses will only give you about 20% to 40% of the melt value. You'd be lucky if you received $4,000.

These businesses are making 100% to 200% instead of a fair margin of perhaps 5% to 15%.

NEVER bring your gold or silver to these types of establishments if you want to be treated fairly.

If you were to sell your scrap metals to My Gold Advisor, you'd receive between 85% and 95% of the melt value. We simply don't believe in gouging people who don't know how to value their old jewelry.

– Bonus –

How do I use my 401K, IRA or QRP to buy precious metals? Can I hold them myself or do they have to be held by someone else?

QUICK:

You can buy gold or silver with *any* retirement account. The difference between using an IRA, a standard 401k, and a QRP is that the IRA (even a self-directed IRA) and the standard 401k require a custodian to hold the assets. **With a QRP (which is a specific type of 401k), you're legally allowed to hold the precious metals yourself.** Many promoters claim you can hold metals in a self-directed IRA, but if you read the tax code and IRS regulations, you'll find the opposite to be true. The only truly safe and secure way to use retirement funds to buy and hold gold and silver is to set up a QRP.

You can roll over your old 401k money into a QRP tax-free and penalty-free. And when you do, you'll have access to those funds with checkbook control. *You* have the power and control with a QRP.

For more information on setting up a QRP: Go to www. TheQRP.org

DIRTY DETAILS:

Section 401 of the IRS Code states very specifically the limitations on what can be purchased with retirement funds.

Anyone with a 401k or an IRA can use those funds to buy gold and silver. You're free to buy gold and silver bullion coins. In fact, you can use a 401k or an IRA to buy almost anything other than a vacation house, collectible rugs, or collectible coins.

The difference between the different accounts is whether you're allowed to hold the gold or silver yourself or whether you're required to hold it at a different facility.

With a QRP, a form of self-directed 401k retirement plan, you can actually hold the gold and silver yourself. You don't have to have a custodian. You aren't required to have the metals held in Delaware or Utah or somewhere else.

You do not have this option with an IRA, even a self-directed IRA. Some IRAs are being promoted with the false claim that the account holder is permitted to hold physical metals, but the advisors spouting these claims are circumventing IRS rules with imaginary loopholes and gimmicky language. They're wrong, and they're putting you in danger.

If you buy gold and silver without a custodian being involved— or the custodian is ignored and you hold the stuff yourself—the IRS could say the transaction is disallowed. If the IRS decides a transaction is disallowed, the penalty is brutal.

The IRS can impose a fine of up to 115% of the value of the asset or transaction. You can literally lose all your money and then some!

To protect yourself and your retirement funds from these penalties, we highly recommend you set up and use a QRP. Setting up a QRP is quick and simple, and it allows you to use your retirement funds to hold your own gold and silver.

Do yourself a favor and look into the QRP by visiting the

www.TheQRP.org.

PART IV

Top 7 Scams

Scam #1:

WIRING—When (or if) to send money to a dealer you don't know

QUICK:

Don't wire money to a dealer you don't trust and know on a first name basis.

DIRTY DETAILS:

The industry standard is to send payment to a dealer for your metals before they ship to you. The same process happens if you use Amazon or eBay. You pay first and then the company ships the product to you.

Although this is standard procedure, it does open you to some risk. What if the dealer doesn't fulfill his end of the deal? When selecting a dealer to work with, the best way to avoid this scam is to use a dealer you've been referred to by a trusted friend or advisor that's done significant business with the dealer and had a consistently great experience.

If you're working with a dealer for the first time that's kind of a mystery, I highly recommend starting with a small order and testing the dealer.

Once you wire your money, there's no way to stop it or get it back. A wire is permanent, and the money is gone. Be careful wiring only to someone you trust implicitly.

Scam #2:

CONFISCATION—Could my gold and silver get confiscated?

QUICK:

There is no reasonable argument for the government to confiscate gold or silver today. The only reason this confiscation thing comes up is because a dealer is trying to sell a customer an overpriced highly marked-up collectible coin. Sketchy dealers try to use the FDR executive order as a scare tactic to get the customer to buy a collectible coin instead of the more rational bullion.

DIRTY DETAILS:

Confiscation is not only unlikely but there is not a single record of it ever happening. Dealers claim FDR confiscated all the gold in America. The truth is, he didn't confiscate any gold at all when he issued his executive order in 1933.

Roosevelt issued an executive order to nationalize gold and made it illegal for Americans to own more than five ounces of gold personally unless it was a collectible coin or they required it for business (jewelry, dentistry, etc.). However, the gold was not confiscated. It was bought and paid for by the federal government. When FDR nationalized gold, Americans were required to turn in their gold in exchange for what was a fair value at the time: $20.67 per ounce.

The government didn't just steal the gold. There were zero cases of the federal government breaking down anyone's door or arresting anyone for holding gold. The confiscation myth is one of the biggest scams propagated by bad dealers. It's a great scare tactic for dealers to sell old gold at outrageous markups. They sell overpriced "non-confiscatable, non-reportable" Double Eagles from the early 20th century to rip off their customers.

"The government might confiscate your gold like it did back in 1933," they say. "We can protect you from that," they say. This is a bold-faced lie, and most of the dealers know it.

No dealer can tell you what the government is going to do in the future and this blatantly false manipulation of FDR's executive order into something it was not is immoral if not criminal.

WHY DID FDR ISSUE THE ORDER?

In 1933 gold was used as money and the dollar was tied to gold. Gold is no longer used as money and we are not on the gold standard. There is simply no reason to confiscate gold; it doesn't make any sense. Another major difference between 1933 and today most U.S. dollars are overseas. If the federal government initiated any type of gold confiscation, this action would wreak havoc on the financial system and likely cause the dollar to collapse overnight.

Back in the 1930s President Roosevelt issued the executive order so the federal government could spend significantly more money than it already was to stimulate the economy. This required the government to devalue to the dollar relative to gold. If all Americans hadn't been required to exchange their gold for paper currency first, the entire plan would have been

CONFISCATION—COULD MY GOLD AND SILVER GET CONFISCATED?

foiled. Americans holding gold would suddenly have been rich, and Americans holding paper currency would suddenly have been poor. This wouldn't just have been unfair but would have caused economic chaos. Everyone had to be forced to switch over to the same money—*i.e.*, the paper currency—first.

The major difference between the 1930s and today is that all the federal government has to do to spend more money is to sell treasury bonds to the Federal Reserve central bank, which in turn fires up the printing press and prints additional fiat dollars* out of thin air, something called the monetization of debt. For more on this, check out G. Edward Griffin's book *The Creature from Jekyll Island*.

Anytime there's a need to devalue the dollar so the federal government can increase spending or spur export activity through lower prices on domestic goods, the Fed can print as many fiat dollars as needed.

Gold doesn't back the currency, so there's no need to require Americans to turn theirs in or sell theirs off for the government to spend more or the Federal Reserve to print more.

In 1933 gold was valued at $20.67 per ounce—by law. Dollars were totally convertible into gold and gold into dollars. FDR wanted to put more money into circulation, but the federal government couldn't magically create more gold. Instead, the federal government simply changed the law so that it could print $35 for every ounce of gold in reserve rather than $20.67. The dollar immediately lost 65% of its purchasing power.

Foreigners were fine because they kept their gold the whole time. They still had the same purchasing power as before.

Americans, on the other hand, got hammered. They'd already traded in their gold for dollars.

The coins' unethical dealer like to sell with this scam are the graded Double Eagles. I like Double Eagles, but only at a fair cost of about 3-5% over spot. They should be sold only at a very small premium over the actual gold in the coin. There are millions of these coins, so they are not exactly rare and unique.

If you can buy these coins for a few percent over the spot price, you're basically paying for the gold in the coin. I don't see anything wrong with this type of deal. It's a great way to buy old gold.

Bottom line: don't pay a giant premium and get screwed so the dealer can get rich off your fear. If most of your money is going to pay for the metal itself, you're buying legitimate gold.

*FIAT DOLLARS OR FIAT CURRENCY:

The term "fiat currency" is a term given to money printed by a central bank or government that is backed by nothing other than faith in the currency. The value of the money is dictated by the government, and citizens are required by law to accept that money and *only that money* as legal tender. The government's say-so is what makes this "money" valuable. Gold and silver are valuable by their nature, not by dictate.

Scam #3:

BAIT & SWITCH—Selling Confusion

QUICK:

If you feel like you're being pitched by a used car salesman and the price of your coins or the story about the coins seems too good to be true, it's probably a classic "bait and switch" con. Once an unethical dealer gets you on the phone, they often try to sell you collectible stuff with higher margins instead of the coins you called them about or the ones they advertised.

DIRTY DETAILS:

A lot of dealers will advertise a coin for less than the spot value or "at dealer cost." But when you get them on the phone, they try to sell you a collectible or a rare coin at a 30% to 100% markup instead. They try to scare you with the "non-confiscatable, non- reportable" nature of the coin. They'll reference the Roosevelt executive order from 1933 (see Scam #2) and claim you're safe.

The coins they're selling are extraordinarily hard to sell back for anywhere near what they're selling them to you for. A great question that most people don't usually think to ask is, "How much will you buy these back from me for?" It's always a fraction of what they're asking.

A legitimate dealer will not hesitate to tell you the difference between what he'll sell you a coin for and what he'll buy it back from you for. This difference is called the spread. It should be

3% to 6%. If the dealer won't say, or if the spread is much more than 6%, this is a serious red flag.

With these allegedly "non-confiscatable" coins, the price of gold typically needs to jump 40% to 60% for you just to break even. How is that good for anyone except the smooth-talking salesman? By the way, their response is usually, "Don't worry about that. You're holding these for three to five years." Why would you want to have to wait a year or two just to break even? You can break even just by hanging up the phone, which is what I recommend you do right away.

Numismatics are collectible and rare by their nature. These types of coins offer something other than just the raw commodity, and these coins always have a story. Many unscrupulous dealers deal heavily in the numismatic world because values are not transparent. They're able to build large margins into the price and make obscene profits while screwing the public.

It's hard to figure out what the real value is for a collectible coin or bar unless you're an expert who deals with them all the time. It's a dangerous place for people to invest if they don't know what they're doing. On the other hand, it's a great place for dealers to make a lot of money!

I'm not a fan of numismatics, and we never play this type of game at My Gold Advisor. If something isn't in our clients' best interest, we won't do it—regardless of how profitable it might be.

The coins to look out for are the Kronas, the British Sovereigns and other international fractional coins (fractional means in sizes less than one ounce). These coins tend to be in odd sizes, making them confusing and hard to compute in terms of value. Most novices should stay far away.

An example of fractional coins could be: the coin is point four ounces and 22 carat gold. How many ounces of gold is in that? Between the odd weight and the less than pure nature of the coin, most investors quickly get lost in the story and have no idea what the coin is even worth. This is a bad idea!

If you're lost in the conversion, transparency and intelligent decisions are gone!

Unethical dealers like to sell confusing coins and create a story around them so the unsuspecting customer falls in love with the story and stops thinking about how much they're overpaying.

One popular story goes like this: "These coins were smuggled out of America after Roosevelt confiscated all the gold. They were hidden in a vault for 80 years, and we just got a hold of them. We only have a few hundred, and you can get in on this before they're gone. Wow! Uncirculated, beautiful, and yours for a limited time." Puke! Don't fall for this! **It's a scam**!

Unscrupulous dealers will work anyone they can with any method of closing possible. They'll fast talk you, confuse you, scare you, compliment you, and even embarrass you. The dealer can make a lot of money, because they're selling you something you don't understand.

I recommend .9999 pure gold like a Gold Maple Leaf or Gold U.S. Buffalo—or stick with an American Eagle, which is 22 carat gold but still contains one full ounce of gold. (The Eagle weighs just over an ounce because of the addition weight of the impurities. These impurities are intentional and make the coin more durable.)

Every American Gold Eagle has one full ounce of gold so the value is easy to compute. The Maple Leafs are my other favorite, very simple and easy to value. There's no mystery about what you're buying or what you have in your portfolio. They are very common, and they're super liquid (easy to sell back to any reputable dealer for cash quickly and easily anywhere on earth).

Scam #4:

BOILER ROOM DEALERS—
High pressure, low value

QUICK:

If you've ever seen the movie *Boiler Room*, you'll understand this scam. In this scam, you have a big room with a bunch of guys calling lists of people and hard selling them on a very rare, very exclusive deal that will be gone soon (an exploding offer).

DIRTY DETAILS:

I worked undercover in a boiler room watching the "brokers" dial all day, talking their poor unsuspecting targets into buying overpriced "specialty coins." The "brokers," as they called themselves, used all sorts of fear tactics to lead their prospects into buying overpriced collectibles and specialty proofs. Over and over, I heard the main broker Brian say, "Sir, I recommend you go with the non-confiscatable, non-reportable Double Eagle." Every time I heard that, I wanted to puke.

They'd often use bogus charts that focused on a specific rare coin that had done well for a narrow period and then used that one example as proof that the rare coin was a better buy than the bullion coins.

The true charts with long-term trends and actual large data samples showed the exact opposite result, but naturally those charts didn't sell collectible coins very well so they were kept in the cabinets away from the target.

I'm calling the customer a "target" on purpose because in my mind someone is a client if I'm working for them and serving them in a fiduciary role, with honesty and integrity. The type of boiler rooms that sell these high markup coins using scare tactics are neither honest nor are they acting with integrity. Their focus is on how much they can sell and pocket that week, target be damned. And there's always a hundred more they are waiting to call.

Watch out for boiler rooms. Best to work with dealers you've been referred to by people you trust and who are financially savvy.

Scam #5:

PYRAMID SCAMS—
The "silver snowball" &
other network marketing cons

QUICK:

This is a classic recruitment scam where you dupe your friends into buying overpriced collectible coins in exchange for free coins of your own. It's a great way to either lose money or lose friends, possibly both.

DIRTY DETAILS:

The Silver Snowball Scam has been pitched to me by customers several times over the past couple of years.

It goes like this: you (the target) buy a couple of silver Eagles each month and recruit others to buy a couple of Eagles as well. For every three people you enroll, you'll get a free eagle each month. Sounds like a great deal—except the price you're paying is 40% over the spot price (which is about four times the premium you should be paying).

This is a great deal for you if you don't have any problem suckering other people into the scam, but unfortunately your recruits get screwed into buying overpriced Eagles just so you can get one for free. This is a classic pyramid scam where the early participants make tons of money with overpriced products but the later participants get crushed when they run out of new blood they can fool into buying the junk.

Here's the math. For this example, let's assume the spot price on silver is $30.

You buy three Eagles for $42 each from Snowball, Inc.

You then recruit three people to do the same. They each buy three Eagles from Snowball, Inc., and you get a free Eagle.

Now you have four Eagles and paid a total of $126. That's an average price of just over $31. The actual fair market value is about $34 for an Eagle. So you've done well—you're getting the Eagles at a 10% discount.

HERE'S HOW YOUR RECRUITS DID:

They bought three Eagles for $42 each and didn't sign anyone up. Their average price is $42 per coin, so they paid 30% more than they would have if they bought them from a reputable dealer. Part of that extra went to subsidize your Eagles, and the rest went to the company running the Silver Snowball Scam.

These pyramid scams always show up in a booming market and are sure to appear in different forms over the next few years as gold and silver continue their upward rise and appreciation.

If it sounds too good to be true, IT IS!

Scam #6:

LEVERAGE—The Interest Trap

QUICK:

The Leverage scam goes like this: You see an ad in a newspaper or magazine saying, "Own $10,000 worth of gold for only $2,000." You call the company, and they tell you they have a deal where you can buy $10,000 worth of gold with only $2,000 down and they'll finance the rest.

DIRTY DETAILS:

Seems great! Since precious metals are rising, you get to juice your returns and use leverage. The first problem with this scam is that you have fees and interest. Whether gold goes up or down, you're paying interest on the borrowed money. If gold goes down just 5%, you would lose 25% of your money instantly and likely have the broker calling you to insist you send more cash over.

The second problem is that you don't get to hold the metals. You've effectively bought a contract (paper gold).

One of the reasons to buy gold and silver is to eliminate the counter-party risk. Buying with leverage seems like a way to get extra return, but there's a reason it's being offered. It's a winner for the dealer. In this case, the dealer is the same as a casino. And just like a casino, the house always wins.

Only buy what you can afford with cash you have—or a 401K, IRA or QRP—to make sure that you aren't getting yourself into an interest trap.

Scam #7:

CASH FOR GOLD STORES— Quick cash at a huge price

QUICK:

The increase in the price of gold and silver over the last twelve years is evident in the explosion of new "cash for gold" stores all over the place. These stores are everywhere! They seem to pop up in every strip mall that has an extra bay open. Why are they popping up and how can so many of them be in business?

These stores buy scrap gold and silver in jewelry and coins. The scam is that they pay pennies and nickels on the dollar. I went into a couple of stores to verify this and was offered 50% of the value of my coins and about 20% of the value of my jewelry.

DIRTY DETAILS:

These stores are open because they're ridiculously profitable, and they're ridiculously profitable because they're ripping people off. When we buy scrap from people at My Gold Advisor, we generally pay 80% to 95% of spot as opposed to the 20% to 50% these stores pay.

The public simply doesn't know how much their gold and silver are worth. Getting cash for old junk they had sitting around sounds great until they realize what the value of gold and silver truly is! Some of these stores are even paying more for coins and jewelry than their customers paid for them 10 years ago, but it's still a rip-off considering gold has risen to six times its value in 2000 and silver has worth 10 times more than it was then. These scam houses are getting away with ripping people off while appearing to be helpful and generous.

I highly encourage you to check the Better Business Bureau website and look into any company you're considering doing business with. Look us up, and check out our A+ rating.

- Conclusion -

T he goal in writing this book was to take the mask off of gold and silver and reveal the truth about precious metals so you have a better shot at protecting your wealth, as well as a better understanding of the truth behind the chaos going on in the financial markets today.

The first part provided an understanding about the reasons gold and silver are valuable and why you should have them in your portfolio to protect your wealth. It explained why you're better off with metals over paper assets like mutual funds, stocks, bonds and annuities, and it explored why you've been lied to by the financial industry about what's really in your best interest.

The second part explained the reason for owning gold and silver now, why the timing is critical, and why delaying could be devastating because of the ongoing financial crisis that is the result of government overspending and the incessant printing of money by central banks—neither of which are likely to stop in the near term.

The third section explained the nuts and bolts of how you buy gold and silver, how you pick and test a dealer, and even how you can use your retirement funds like an IRA or 401k to purchase and hold physical gold and silver. And the final section provided you with the red flags and warning signs of potential scams so you can recognize and run away from a disreputable dealer if you come across one.

I hope you've found value in the information provided in this book and have a stronger understanding of how to protect your wealth with gold and silver.

Please consider sharing this book with others you care about to help them protect their wealth.

Thank you for investing your time with this book.

~ Damion S. Lupo

- Summary & Services -

BUYING AND SELLING GOLD & SILVER

If you're interested in purchasing gold or silver, please call us and one of our partners will provide you with world class service. Our primary objective is to educate you and answer all of your questions before we do business together.

The QRP

For additional information on setting up a QRP or using retirement funds including a 401k or IRA to purchase precious metals, please call us or visit us online.

Visit www.TheQRP.org

You'll get immediate access to the audiobook and be able to subscribe to the monthly email newsletter. The newsletter includes time-sensitive news you can use to protect your wealth, plus insider information on gold and silver.

For anything else, please contact us:

Email info@mygoldadvisor.com

Call 800.846.6280

Visit www.MyGoldAdvisor.com

Happy Hedging!

- Recommended Resources -

BOOKS

The Q.R.P.—Damion S. Lupo

Rich Dad's Guide to Gold & Silver—Mike Maloney

The ABCs of Gold Investing—Michael Kosares

Get the Skinny on Silver Investing—David Morgan

WORLD CLASS DEALERS

My Gold Advisor www.MyGoldAdvisor.com

Marc Watts & Gaithersburg Coin Exchange www.gaithersburg coinexchange.com

AMARK www.amark.com

American Precious Metals www.APMEX.com

Kitco www.kitco.com